Korea
after
Kim Jong-il

Korea
after
Kim Jong-il

Marcus Noland

Institute for International Economics
Washington, DC
January 2004

Marcus Noland, senior fellow, was a senior economist in the Council of Economic Advisers and held research or teaching positions at the Johns Hopkins University, the University of Southern California, Tokyo University, Saitama University, the University of Ghana, the Korea Development Institute, and the East-West Center. He received fellowships sponsored by the Japan Society for the Promotion of Science, the Council on Foreign Relations, the Council for the International Exchange of Scholars, and the Pohang Iron and Steel Corporation. He won the 2001–02 Ohira Masayoshi Award for his book *Avoiding the Apocalypse: The Future of the Two Koreas* (2000). He is the editor of *Economic Integration of the Korean Peninsula* (1998) and coauthor of *Industrial Policy in an Era of Globalization: Lessons from Asia* (2003), *No More Bashing: Building a New Japan–United States Economic Relationship* (2001), *Global Economic Effects of the Asian Currency Devaluations* (1998), and *Reconcilable Differences? United States–Japan Economic Conflict* (1993).

INSTITUTE FOR INTERNATIONAL
ECONOMICS
1750 Massachusetts Avenue, NW
Washington, DC 20036-1903
(202) 328-9000 FAX: (202) 659-3225
http://www.iie.com

C. Fred Bergsten, *Director*
Valerie Norville, *Director of Publications
    and Web Development*
Brett Kitchen, *Director of Marketing*

*Printing by Kirby Lithographic Company, Inc.
Typesetting by Sandra F. Watts*

Printed in the United States of America
06 05 04   5 4 3 2 1

Library of Congress Cataloging-in-Publication Data

Noland, Marcus, 1959–
    Korea after Kim Jong-il / Marcus Noland.
        p. cm.
    Includes bibliographical references and index.
        ISBN 0-88132-373-X
        1. Korea (North)—Economic conditions.
2. Korea (North)—Politics and government.   3. Korea (North)—Foreign economic relations.   4. Korea (North)—Foreign relations.   5. Korea (North)—Foreign economic relations—Korea (South).   6. Korea (South)—Foreign economic relations—Korea (North).   7. Korea—Economic integration.   8. Korean reunification question (1945–).   9. Kim, Chœong-il, 1942–.   I. Institute for International Economics (U.S.).   II. Title.

HC470.2.N65 2003
330.9519—dc22

                    2003065585

Contents

Preface   vii

Acknowledgments   xi

1   Political Change in North Korea   1
    Abrupt Political Change, or Is North Korea
      a (Pre) Revolutionary Society?   2
    The (Non) Collapse of North Korea   12

2   Modeling Regime Change   21
    Background on Modeling   28
    Results   33

3   Transition Paths   43
    July 2002 Reforms   46
    Gradual Integration   57
    "Radical" Integration   63

4   Implications for South Korea   71
    The Economics of Engagement   72
    Final Thoughts   83

Data Appendix   85

References   89

Index   97

Tables

Table 2.1   Economic declines, 1960–2001   23
Table 2.2   Economic downturns in selected long-lived regimes   26
Table 2.3   Hazard regressions   35
Table A.1   Estimates for North Korea, 1990–2002   87

Figures

Figure 2.1   North Korean GDP growth, 1990–2002   22
Figure 2.2   Cumulative hazards   37
Figure 2.3   Hazard of regime change, 1990–2002   39
Figure 2.4   Hazard of regime change under three scenarios, 1990–2003   40

Preface

Despite the passage of 50 years since an armistice ended military hostilities, the Korean peninsula remains divided, a Cold War vestige that seemingly has been unaffected by the evolution that has occurred elsewhere. If anything, the United States' confrontation with North Korea—a charter member of its "axis of evil"—has intensified in recent years. At the same time, North Korea has begun economic reforms, which, whatever their ultimate impact on the North Korean economy, have moved the country from the realm of the elite to mass politics, fundamentally raising the stakes in terms of the North's internal political stability.

The situation is enormously complex. Today's North Korean regime embodies elements of both communism and Confucian dynasty. It is sovereign with respect to only part of the divided Korean nation. It is vulnerable to pressure from external powers. It confronts incipient internal demands for change. The polity has unclear rules for political succession and is in the midst of far-reaching reforms of its economy and reinterpretation of its motivating ideology of *juche* or self-reliance. Given the country's strategic location and questions about its nuclear weapons program, whether the current leadership will be able to successfully navigate these political and economic shoals is an open question of extraordinary global importance.

Korea after Kim Jong-il examines the medium- to long-run economic and political outlook for North Korea. Author Marcus Noland develops a path-breaking quantitative analysis of the probability of regime change and the influence of foreign countries on such prospects, explores the character of possible successor regimes, and analyzes the implications of these profoundly different trajectories for South Korea. The study concludes that the survival of the Kim Jong-il regime strongly depends on the support of outside powers, most importantly South Korea. It then analyzes in detail the potential impact on South Korea of both gradual and abrupt economic integration with the North, concluding that the South remains highly vulnerable to developments in the North.

Noland's previous book on Korea for the Institute, *Avoiding the Apocalypse: The Future of the Two Koreas* (2000), won the prestigious Ohira Masayoshi Memorial Prize for best book on Asia in 2001–02 and is part of a research program on Korea without parallel beyond the peninsula. Among the Institute's recent publications on Korea are *Industrial Policy in an Era of Globalization: Lessons from Asia* (2003) by Marcus Noland and Howard Pack; *The Korean Diaspora in the World Economy* (2003), edited by C. Fred Bergsten and Inbom Choi; and *Free Trade between Korea and the United States?* (2001) by Inbom Choi and Jeffrey J. Schott.

The Institute for International Economics is a private nonprofit institution for the study and discussion of international economic policy. Its purpose is to analyze important issues in that area and to develop and communicate practical new approaches for dealing with them. The Institute is completely nonpartisan.

The Institute is funded largely by philanthropic foundations. Major institutional grants are now being received from the William M. Keck, Jr. Foundation and the Starr Foundation. A number of other foundations and private corporations contribute to the highly diversified financial resources of the Institute. About 18 percent of the Institute's resources in our latest fiscal year were provided by contributors outside the United States, including about 8 percent from Japan.

The Board of Directors bears overall responsibilities for the Institute and gives general guidance and approval to its research program, including the identification of topics that are likely to become important over the medium run (one to three years), and which should be addressed by the Institute. The director, working closely with the staff and outside Advisory Committee, is responsible for the development of particular projects and makes the final decision to publish an individual study.

The Institute hopes that its studies and other activities will contribute to building a stronger foundation for international economic policy around the world. We invite readers of these publications to let us know how they think we can best accomplish this objective.

C. Fred Bergsten
Director
December 2003

Acknowledgments

I would like to thank Paul E. Karner for research assistance and Oh Seungyoun for translation assistance. The research with which they assisted me was transformed into the actual book that you are holding by Madona Devasahayam and Marla Banov of the Institute publications department with good cheer and in record time.

Political Change in North Korea

Recently a Korean journalist repeatedly asked me whether I would prefer a "radical" or "gradual" economic integration between North and South Korea.[1] I replied that whether they experienced an abrupt process of integration along the lines of Germany or the gradual, consensual integration that both governments profess to desire would largely be a function of North Korea's internal regime dynamics—my preference was immaterial in this regard.

In a sense this policy analysis is an attempt to provide a more informative answer to that possibly ill-specified question. The nature of the current regime, embodying elements of both communism and Confucian dynasty; its sovereign status with respect to only part of the divided Korean nation; its vulnerability to pressure from larger external powers; and its confrontation with the incipient demands for internal social, political, and economic change driven by its isolation as a socialist island in a capitalist sea generate an unusually broad set of possible transition paths and successor regimes. Such paths range from effective maintenance of the status quo to evolution, probably toward a more conventional form of military authoritarianism, to revolutionary upheaval, in all likelihood implying the North's collapse and its absorption into the rival Southern state.

The title of this policy analysis is intentionally provocative. North Korea's present leader, Kim Jong-il, son of the country's charismatic founding leader Kim Il-sung, is more than 60 years old and reputedly not in the best of health (even discounting a history of South Korean disinformation campaigns on this point). It is possible that he may successfully manage

---

1. Throughout this policy analysis, for simplicity's sake, the Republic of Korea will be referred to as South Korea and the Democratic People's Republic of Korea as North Korea.

a transition from ruling to reigning. (Former US Secretary of State Madeleine Albright [2003] reports that he communicated interest in "the Thai model" during their October 2000 meeting.) It is possible that he will successfully conclude an unprecedented third generational transfer of power to one or another of his sons, though the lack of public propaganda campaigns to lay the groundwork for such a succession or apparent absence of his sons from high-level policymaking should give pause. The July 2002 initiation of economic reforms—affecting the lives of all North Koreans at the grass-roots level—has raised the stakes politically, and other outcomes—abrupt transition to non-Kim family leadership with or without *juche* (the near-theological ideology of national self-reliance), collapse, or civil war—are possible as well. Associated with these distinct political trajectories are equally diverse paths of economic development, carrying with them profoundly different implications for the future of the North Korean economy and its integration with its neighbors, most importantly South Korea.

The policy analysis begins with some reflections on the nature of political change in general and the now voluminous literature on the "collapse" of the North Korean regime in particular. The question is then posed, whether on the basis of our understanding of the determinants of political change, were those who predicted (and in some cases continue to predict) abrupt political change in North Korea correct to do so, despite the fact that it has not materialized? Put another way, on the basis of our understanding of regime dynamics, were the "collapsists" correct to predict abrupt change (hence the regime's durability is unusual or unexpected), or is the continuing existence of the Kim family regime in the North actually what one would expect on the basis of formal modeling (i.e., the expectations of collapse were misguided)?

The policy analysis then takes up the issue of what the most likely form of regime change would be, if it were to occur. This gives us the basis to then address the essence of the reporter's question: What are the likelihoods of "radical" and "gradual" economic integration and what are the welfare implications of these alternative paths?

Abrupt Political Change, or Is North Korea a (Pre) Revolutionary Society?

In discussions of North Korea, the term "collapse" is frequently invoked, though seldom defined.[2] One can define collapse in multiple ways: in

---

2. The term "collapse" is often used loosely. Huh (1996), S.C. Kim (1996), and Pollack and Lee (1999) are laudable exceptions. Foster-Carter (1997b) contains a rigorous application to North Korea of multiple-level crises (systemic—economic and rationality—and identity [subjective]—legitimation and motivation) based on the work of Frankfurt School philosopher Jürgen Habermas, well beyond the reach of this study.

terms of a collapse of the economy, a collapse of the political regime, and ultimately the collapse and disappearance of North Korea as a sovereign state. Economists normally don't use the term, and it carries no technical meaning.[3] One might define collapse as a process of economic disintegration that reduces the value of output below the level required to sustain a population biologically. On this definition, given the allocative preferences of the Kim Jong-il regime (i.e., its massive expenditures on the military), the aid-dependent North Korean economy "collapsed" sometime during the 1990s, though the regime and the state did not.

Likewise the term "regime," though subject to multiple and imprecise definitions, is a similarly loosely and overused term in discussions of North Korea.[4] In academic discourse, "regime" typically denotes a set of political norms and principles embodied in a set of formal and informal procedural rules and institutions governing access to and the use of state power, often resting on a particular set of constituencies, classes, or social groups. In this sense, regime normally is not associated with particular incumbents—that is, an electoral defeat for US President George W. Bush in November 2004 and the accession to office of his duly elected opponent in January 2005 would not be considered a "regime change."

This usual distinction between incumbent and regime raises difficult issues in the case of North Korea, which is historically unique in its political culture, fusing totalitarian and dynastic attributes embodied in a deified familial leadership. In their formal model of regime dynamics, Bruce Bueno de Mesquita and Jongryn Mo (1997, 25–27) concluded that unless he successfully co-opted the Korean People's Army (KPA), Kim Jong-il could be rendered "little more than a titular leader" or "figurehead" in a military-dominated system. Indeed, it is precisely the possibility of the rise to power of a (possibly reformist) military authoritarian–governing coalition—a North Korean Park Chung-hee or Augusto Pinochet who could make the trains run on time (or in the case of North Korea, simply run at all)—that has animated much of the thinking about post-Kim North Korea (Scalapino 1992a, 1992b, 1995; Ahn 1994a, 1994b; Lho 1999).

This vision is based on a series of unexamined assumptions. Is the maintenance of such a post-*juche* regime conceivable, or rather, is the whole raison d'être of the North Korean state so bound up in *juche* ideology that the disappearance of the Kim family regime would be

---

3. One, and possibly the only, exception is Hirshleifer (1963), who defines economic collapse as "a failure in the mode of functioning of the economic system, in essence, a breakdown in the division of labor . . . so that production [falls] even more than [do] the resources available" (p. 113). The problem with this definition is that it would seem to encompass any major fall in aggregate demand whether or not it was accompanied by increases in mortality or systemic changes.

4. On the first point, see the appendix in Munck (1996) for a compendium of alternate definitions of "regime."

tantamount to the collapse and disappearance of the North Korean state? Or is it possible to have *juche* without the Kims? Is the ideology sufficiently open-ended and amenable to reinterpretation that it could be used to legitimate a post-Kim reformist regime? Does the current "military-first politics" campaign with its emphasis on modernization represent the embryonic start of such a reinterpretation?[5] How does the existence of South Korea complicate this process of legitimization? What if South Korea sought to promote such a government as an alternative to collapse and absorption along German lines? Or does the extreme degree of politicization of North Korean society preclude any transitional path save revolutionary political change, thereby reducing the likelihood of a stable and permanent successor regime? That is to say, rather than the hoped-for North Korean Park Chung-hee or Augusto Pinochet, would Kim's successor more likely be a North Korean Alexander Kerensky, Mehdi Barzagan, or Lothar de Maizière—political moderates who were swept awry by revolutionary upheaval in Russia, Iran, and East Germany, respectively?

In his 1968 masterpiece, *Political Order in Changing Societies*, Samuel P. Huntington defines revolution as "a rapid, fundamental, and violent domestic change in dominant values and myths of a society, in its political institutions, social structure, leadership, and government activities and policies" produced by the inability of governing institutions to cope with the swift rise in political consciousness of new groups and their precipitate mobilization into politics (Huntington 1968, 264). In complete revolutions, this first upheaval phase is followed by the "creation and institutionalization of a new political order. The successful revolution combines rapid political mobilization and rapid political institutionalization" (Huntington 1968, 266).[6] Of course, this is not the only definition of revolution. Theda Skocpol (1979) argues that revolutions involve an inevitable strengthening of the state. Under this definition, the possibility of revolution in North Korea, at least in its functioning pre-1990 form, is almost ruled out. Whether there could be a revolutionary reconstitution of the North Korean state from its current degraded form is an open question.

Huntington goes on to distinguish between two types of revolutions—a "Western" revolution in which the collapse of the governing institutions is followed by the mobilization of new groups and the construction

---

5. Bruce Cumings (1995, 1997) makes the interesting point that unlike Mao Tse-tung, Kim Il-sung did not disparage intellectuals; he in fact gave them symbolic representation in the Korean Workers Party (KWP) emblem. This acceptance of technical competence as a virtue might facilitate a modernizing reinterpretation of *juche*.

6. Charles Tilly (1978) extends this analysis to focus on specific groups contending for state power, their ability to mobilize (broadly defined) resources, and the state's ability to satisfy or resist these demands. One of the curious features of North Korean society is that due to the prolonged period of extreme militarization of the society, now lasting more than two generations, there are a lot of people in North Korean society with military training and skill, should an insurgent group ever contest power.

of a new political order (along the lines of the French, Russian, Cuban, and Iranian revolutions) and an "Eastern" revolution in which the mobilization of new groups and the creation of alternative, rival institutions ends in the violent overthrow of the incumbent regime, as occurred in the Chinese and Vietnamese revolutions. If North Korea is to experience revolution, it is unlikely to be of the Eastern variety, despite its location.

To this taxonomy one might add one more species, what Barrington Moore Jr. calls "revolutions from above," two major examples being the Meiji Restoration in Japan and the Turkish revolution of the 1920s (Trimberger 1978). Three conditions are necessary: a perceived foreign military threat, a group of ruling elites with no stake in the status quo organization of economic life, and the spread of an ideology, typically nationalism, that elevates modernization as a value to build national strength and avoid foreign domination. Under such circumstances, some faction of the existing elite moves against the regime in order to preserve national sovereignty. Since the dissenters typically include at least part of the military establishment, there is less of a need to mobilize the masses, since the challengers already at least partly control the coercive machinery.

Moreover, the nationalism of the revolutionaries contains appeals couched in terms of traditional institutions and values, indeed, sometimes depicted as being restorative in nature. At the same time, the existence of a foreign threat discourages a complete military showdown between the incumbents and the challengers. For all these reasons, these "revolutions from above" typically involve less social upheaval and are of a shorter duration than the classic revolutions of Huntington's analysis. Indeed, one could question whether these are revolutions at all, narrowly defined. But our concern is with political change in North Korea—whether it is revolutionary in the classical sense or not—not revolution per se, so it is worth keeping this model in mind.[7]

So, is North Korea a prerevolutionary society? One can identify political and social characteristics of societies and political regimes susceptible to revolutionary change and the presence or absence of specific precursors to revolutionary situations. In terms of the institutional prerequisites for revolution, North Korea is intriguing precisely because of its mix of communism and Confucianism, together with the ambiguous role of nationalism and by extension South Korea, because of the stresses placed on the society by its anomalous position in the world system, and because of the high level of latent military skills in the population potentially beyond state control.

"Western" revolutions are typically aimed at highly centralized states, especially those largely based on personal patronage, often headed by a

---

7. And of course there is nothing sacrosanct about these analytical categories—the Ethiopian revolution, for example, appears to have combined aspects of "Eastern," "Western," and "top-down" revolutions into one bloody, protracted struggle.

monarch or dominated by a landed aristocracy. As Jack A. Goldstone (1986, 9) writes, "Because the government is bound up with the person of the chief executive, the crumbling of the patronage network combined with even limited popular uprising can bring the collapse of the entire regime." Political change in such polities may be revolutionary when it combines the breakthrough of the proletariat (Marx), the former landless peasants of the lumpenproletariat (Fanon), or the urban middle class (intellectuals, professionals, and bourgeoisie—Huntington) with the mass mobilization of the peasantry or some non-class-based contending group (Tilly), possibly led by a revolutionary vanguard (Lenin). Absent this combination of forces, political change may occur and generate a variety of outcomes, but revolution is not one of them. Economic modernization and shifting demographics have probably led to a relative decline of rural interests in this equation. Ironically, if Huntington is correct and it really is the urban professional and middle class that counts, then by its very success and emphasis on industrialization, Stalinism created the seeds of its own downfall.

Whether the North Korean middle class or proletariat (lumpen or not) exists in a voiceless premodern state is debatable. Pyongyang accounts for perhaps a quarter of the nonrural population, excluding the military, and the Kim family regime has assiduously catered to the needs of its residents. An additional, though unknown, share of the non-Pyongyang urban population should probably be classified as similarly privileged and presumably lacking in the potential for revolutionary consciousness. The North Koreans have done their own internal assessments of political reliability, and the share deemed reliable is relatively small, on the order of one-quarter of the population, with a core elite of perhaps 200,000, or roughly 1 percent of the population.[8] Unlike the situation in Eastern Europe, where the educated urban population exhibited little loyalty when it became apparent that the Soviets would not use force to back their satellite regimes, the North Korean elite appears to be relatively coherent— many are either blood relatives or descendents of guerrillas who fought with Kim Il-sung, and they recognize that as a class they would have no real role in a unified Korea (Lankov 2003).

Whether the mobilization of the remaining nonelite urban population would be sufficient to affect revolutionary change is unknowable a priori.[9] However, the case of Romania, in which ethnic-based civil unrest in the provincial city of Timişoara (the country's fifth largest, with a population of less than 400,000) sparked the end of the Ceauşescu regime, is a

---

8. On North Korea's internal classification system, see Foster-Carter (1994), Hunter (1999), and Armstrong (2002).

9. See Kuran (1989, 1995a, 1995b) on the issues of preference falsification and the unanticipated nature of political revolutions.

reminder that sparks can start prairie fires. That said, the specifically ethnic dimension of the Romanian case is absent in North Korea.

In assessing its revolutionary potential, contemporary North Korea may more closely resemble countries that have experienced "revolution from above." There is a perceived foreign threat, and it would not be difficult to imagine intraelite dissent over the incumbent regime's apparent ineptness in dealing with the country's economic troubles. (North Korea is a kind of Rorschach test for social scientists: Political scientists see clever tactics that have parlayed a hole in the ground into a multibillion dollar aid consortium—the Korean Peninsula Energy Development Organization (KEDO); economists see policy barbarism.) Current propaganda that emphasizes "military-first" politics to build a "powerful and prosperous country" out of the "barrel of a gun" oddly echoes the "wealthy nation and a strong army" slogan of Meiji-era Japan. One could imagine this militarized nationalism being used to remove the current leadership in favor of a more technically competent group of nationalist modernizers.

Prior to the collapse of East Germany (which among communist polities might be regarded as sui generis due to the issue of national division) and later the Soviet Union, no revolution had ever occurred in a communist polity, as it was thought that the highly institutionalized nature of communist politics played a similar role to modern democratic institutions in absorbing and channeling the political demands of new actors. (Modern democracies seldom, if ever, experience revolution because well-functioning democratic institutions are able to accommodate the political demands of new groups and assimilate them into the existing institutional order before rising aspirations reach the point of revolutionary mobilization.)

In the case of Eastern Europe, rising levels of education and urbanization had created a disaffected, if compliant, population. Yet it took economic stagnation, the Soviet defeat in Afghanistan, political mobilization in Poland, and Mikhail Gorbachev's loss of nerve to send the dominoes tumbling down. The events of 1989 in a sense ratified the essential correctness of Leonid Brezhnev's freezing of reform in 1968—rather than reviving the system, the liberalization permitted under Gorbachev simply intensified its contradictions and led to its collapse (Chirot 1996, Przeworski et al. 2000). No utopian dreams were shattered. The populations had long stopped believing the propaganda, if they ever did.

The challenge then was to complete the revolution by reconstituting the state. The problem for Gorbachev's successors was that having inherited a huge and largely dysfunctional state, there was a need to simultaneously reduce the state's role in the economy, while at the same time strengthening its ability to act as an effective and efficient arbiter of the rules of the game. Paradoxically, democratic capitalism, with its emphasis on autonomous firms and households, actually requires a strong state to work—strong in the sense that it is capable of resisting the demands of particularistic interest groups in the name of some broader social interest, not just coercing a compliant populace.

In some cases, largely those nations of Central Europe for whom national identity did not have to be created and for whom the geographical and cultural access to the capitalist democracies was the greatest succeeded; their mirror images—the newly created states of Central Asia—largely did not. Russia itself became the model for what was variously described as "apparatchik capitalism," "markets without institutions," and "anarcholiberalism."

In retrospect, the Eastern European experience suggests that while Leninist regimes are characterized by a high level of political institutionalization, the omnipresent penetration of politics throughout all aspects of social life and the tendency toward centralization in these regimes create revolutionary vulnerabilities. Certainly, communist polities have a revealed susceptibility to the decay that is the first stage of "Western" revolution. The historical results with respect to the rapid creation of new institutions are ambiguous or mixed—in some cases the rapid creation of the institutions of modern democracy completed the revolution (Czech Republic, Poland, and Hungary), while in others noncommunist successor regimes (Belarus, Turkmenistan, and Uzbekistan) denied revolution by effectively retaining Soviet institutions. In the case of North Korea, the apparent withering of the Korean Workers Party (KWP) and Kim Jong-il's increasing identification with (and reliance on?) the military as an institution of governance suggests a degree of decay that could create revolutionary potential. The issue is ultimately whether North Korea is a "strong" or "weak" state.

Revolutionary change cannot be achieved without mass mobilization, and this typically requires some appeal to nationalism or the spur of foreign intervention. In Eastern Europe this was another factor that weighed against the revolution-inhibiting nature of the Leninist regimes; a significant share of the populace always regarded them as an alien Soviet imposition. Ironically, it was communism's success at creating a literate, urban population that created its problems. Unlike China with its vast reservoirs of politically docile peasants with whom to fill the ranks of the military, the armies of Central Europe were unreliable politically in terms of internal coercion. Once it became apparent that the Soviets would not back their local satellites militarily, the game was up.

In the case of North Korea, the Kim dynasty appears to have much more effectively fused its *juche* ideology with Korean nationalism, so that nationalism would not appear to be a revolutionary motivation though the current appeals to "military-first" ideology, which is portrayed as emanating from *juche* thought, might create the intellectual leeway to get the current regime or its successor off the *juche* hook. Indeed, the regime uses nationalism as a tool to deflect discontent onto hostile foreign forces. However, it is possible that appeals to unrequited nationalism could undermine an attempt by some future post-Kim strong-man to legitimate a non–Kim Il-sungist state: after all, once *juche* is aban-doned, why be a third-rate South Korean when you can be the real thing?

And, as the experience of Eastern Europe has shown, legitimacy of postcommunist successor regimes is a key issue in their subsequent suc-cess. The reduction of the state's overarching role in the economy re-quires painful reforms, which can be undertaken only if the government is regarded as legitimate. This then sets up a kind of vicious circle: to be effective the government must be legitimate, but to be legitimate it must be effective (Holmes 1996, Skidelsky 1996).

On the other hand, what might be the result if South Korea actively tried to prop up such a leadership in a bid to avert a North Korean collapse and the associated costs of unification? In theory, several of North Korea's neighbors have the economic wherewithal to do the job. (By Chinese standards, North Korea, with its population of 22 million, is a relatively small province.) Yet it is South Korea's response that is key—whatever its pretensions, *juche* is ultimately a nationalist ideology.

In sum, both the dynastic and Leninist aspects of the North Korea polity appear susceptible to revolutionary change. The role of national-ism would seem to augur against it, but the divided-nation aspect of North Korea's existence would also appear to make it more difficult for a post-*juche* nonrevolutionary leadership to use nationalism to establish political legitimacy.

So it is at least conceivable that North Korea today meets the prereq-uisites of a prerevolutionary polity. What is the likelihood of revolution? After all, as Nicholas Eberstadt (1998) points out, not every prerevolutionary state produces a revolution; indeed, few do. Does North Korea today exhibit the characteristics or drivers of a prerevolutionary state? The ex-isting literature suggests a number of revolutionary precursors, beyond the institutional features of the polity already discussed. The first is eco-nomic distress, though the role of economic factors in creating revolu-tionary situations is a complex one. Rich and prosperous countries do not typically experience revolutions, nor do grindingly poor countries. (Contrary to much of the commentary on North Korea during the 1990s famine, countries in the midst of famines never produce revolutions, though famines are sometimes a by-product of social disruptions caused by revo-lutions.) Instead, political instability occurs in modernizing countries that may have experienced a slowdown in growth or deterioration in eco-nomic performance following an earlier period of development. Growth produces social dislocation and anomie (often associated with urbaniza-tion) and may give rise to deepening inequality and associated tensions. Most important, it contributes to rising expectations. The subsequent in-ability to meet those expectations creates social frustrations that may manifest themselves in various forms of violence, civil unrest, and, in extreme cases, revolutionary political mobilization.

Whether those rising social tensions are translated into criminality, political instability, or revolution depends importantly on the ability of the incumbent regime to maintain its legitimacy, which in turn involves retaining the allegiance of the elite and the sanctity of and control over the symbolic interpretation of "national myths" (Brinton 1966, Eberstadt 1998). What is at stake is who will establish the psychopolitical context for the interpretation of the objective conditions of material reality. Defection of the elite (or the seizure of interpretive leadership by vanguard revolutionaries) and loss of control over the interpretation of national myths increase the likelihood that the mass interpretation will occur in ways inimical to the interests of the incumbent regime.

In the extreme, mass mobilization occurs. Whether this is translated into revolutionary upheaval depends on the degree of alienation of key social classes: either the proletariat, lumpenproletariat, urban middle class, or some other urban social identity group, together with the peasantry; and the degree of unanimity among the urban and rural insurgents in support of a common cause. Mass mobilization of key groups is a necessary but not sufficient condition for revolution—to achieve revolution there must be an adequate degree of consensus around the revolutionary program. (The real contribution of Lenin was not in promoting communism as a motivating ideology—it is too limiting for that—but rather Leninism as a mechanism for creating new institutions to consolidate political power.) In the absence of sufficient consensus around programmatic goals, widespread political mobilization may generate political instability or change, but it will not be revolutionary change. Likewise, mass mobilization of one group or another in the absence of more general rise in political mobilization can also give rise to nonrevolutionary political change.

A final and necessary manifestation of this process is the inability to use the state's security forces to put down popular insurrections either due to a disintegration or loss of cohesion of the security institutions or due to the withdrawal of their allegiance from the incumbent regime. This was a key problem for the Soviet client states of Eastern Europe—the national militaries were unreliable for internal purposes. In the case of North Korea, Kim Jong-il assiduously courts the military's needs, and it appears loyal to the regime. The fundamental problem remains, however. During the 1990s famine, leave was suspended to prevent troops from returning to famine-stricken home villages, and there is at least one documented case of a mutiny or attempted coup in 1995 by significant elements of the VI Corps, which was subsequently reorganized. It is not without cause that one close observer described the commanding general of the Pyongyang Defense Command as "the most monitored individual in the country." This is simply to say that the political loyalty of the KPA cannot be taken as given, independent of circumstances.

Whether these preconditions are met and revolution occurs is affected importantly by the quality of the incumbent leadership and their ability to make timely and coherent strategic decisions. Eberstadt (1998) contains interesting case studies of revolutions that did not occur, including in post-Franco Spain and postapartheid South Africa. However, the present North Korean regime does not appear to stack up very well against the examples that Eberstadt cites of political leaderships that managed to successfully avert revolution and instead achieved relatively smooth transitions to constitutional democracies, though in fairness to all concerned it may be difficult to distinguish between system-preserving and system-transforming (or revolution-averting or revolution-facilitating) policy changes in real time.

In the case of Spain, for example, Francisco Franco could not really create a totalitarian regime due to the counterweight of the Catholic Church, and as early as 1959, he began signaling his regime's acceptance of international norms with Spain's accession to membership in various international organizations such as the International Monetary Fund, the Organization for Economic Cooperation and Development, and the European Economic Community. The difference with contemporary North Korea is striking: there is no alternative moral pole (though the existence of democratic and capitalist South Korea may create cognitive dissonance), and North Korea under the Kims has evinced little interest in adhering to international norms across an enormous range of issues, and indeed, might be best thought of as an "alienated state" with no stake in the status quo of international relations (Roy 1998).[10]

Similarly, in the case of South Africa, both key institutions within the society and key leaders acted in ways to avert revolutionary upheaval. To cite a few examples: whatever his motivations, the behavior of P.W. Botha upon his accession to the premiership in 1979 did not seem to place an overwhelming weight on the maintenance of his own personal political power or position. The contrast with Kim Jong-il would appear rather stark in this regard. Institutionally, the Dutch Reformed Church repudiated their scriptural basis of apartheid in 1986—eight years before Nelson Mandela's accession to power. No such disavowal of *juche* appears in train. (Indeed, such a disavowal would appear to be impossible, though perhaps its doctrine might be reinterpreted.)

The apartheid-era South African government's primary political adversary in this regard was the African National Congress (ANC), a multiracial

---

10. A few examples should suffice to establish North Korea's alienation from international norms: its status as the first (and only) country to withdraw from the Nuclear Non-Proliferation Treaty, its status as the first (and only) country to be formally censured by the Convention on International Trade in Endangered Species for repeatedly using diplomatic pouches to smuggle endangered species parts, its state involvement in illegal drug trafficking, and its disinterest in joining the International Labor Organization or adhering to that body's prohibitions on the use of slave labor.

organization that had a long-standing commitment to a nonracial South Africa and a relatively brief history of political violence. Its leader was Nelson Mandela, the closest thing I have ever seen to a secular saint. In contrast, in North Korea there is no ANC and no Mandela. There is no institution capable of constructively channeling mass discontent, and in many respects contemporary North Korea appears more similar to Romania than South Africa (Noland 2000, chapter 9). So while it is possible to point to instances of "averted revolutions" in contemporary history, the resemblance to North Korea today would appear strained.

Indeed, the case of North Korea poses some very basic issues with regard to political transitions. Under what circumstances could the collapse of a communist regime be nonrevolutionary? Communist societies are so thoroughly politicized that the collapse of the political order would seem to imply almost by definition a reordering of almost all aspects of life. Yet some parts of the former Soviet Union (Belarus, Turkmenistan, and Uzbekistan) appear to have jettisoned the ideological commitment to socialism while retaining the Leninist political machinery. And it is possible that in the future, China, Vietnam, Cuba, or North Korea will exhibit nonrevolutionary transitions, if they are not under way already, by "decommunizing" or "depoliticizing" their societies sufficiently to make a relatively smooth transition to postcommunism possible. Or is North Korea more likely to experience abrupt political change?

The (Non) Collapse of North Korea

Numerous observers have predicted the collapse of North Korea since the death of the country's founding leader Kim Il-sung in July 1994, when the life expectancy of the regime that he founded was calculated in months if not weeks,[11] though these commentators had disparate expectations as to what might follow and whether such regime change should be desired or encouraged.[12] The "collapsist" view was widely held in both

---

11. Indeed, some predictions of collapse preceded the death of Kim Il-sung. British sociologist Aidan Foster-Carter, for example, broke the cardinal rule of economic punditry by predicting both an outcome and a date, writing "Korea will be reunified; certainly by 2000; probably 1995; possibly much sooner" (Foster-Carter 1992, 96) and "Economic contraction at around 5 percent annually must eventually precipitate an explosion and collapse of the economy . . . this will trigger political protest and action, in either or both of two forms—an inter-elite coup, probably military, or grassroots protests. Either way, the North Korean regime will be overthrown. As in Germany, there will then be a strong popular demand for immediate integration. This will be irresistible" (Foster-Carter 1994, 32). See Choi (1998) for a more comprehensive survey of regime dynamics.

12. Foster-Carter, for example, has consistently argued that the risks outweigh the benefits, in this regard reflecting the dominant view among the South Korean public, apparently intimidated by the perceived economic costs of German unification (Foster-Carter

scholarly and official circles and also among the South Korean public. The American analyst Nicholas Eberstadt, for example, wrote, "There is little reason at present to expect a reign by Kim Jong-il to be either stable or long" (Eberstadt 1995, 139).[13] South Korean scholar and diplomat Kim Kyung-won in an article titled "No Way Out: North Korea's Impending Collapse" wrote, "[T]here is a real possibility that Kim Jong-il may find himself on the way out in the next few years, pushed out by reformists or military hardliners. More likely, if he is forced out it will be by a coalition of different elements united in one thing only: the judgment that Kim Jong-il is incompetent" (K.W. Kim 1996). His assessment was shared by fellow academic Ahn Byung-joon who predicted that the Kim family regime would be "short-lived," probably followed by a reformist military coup or a break-up and disappearance of the North Korean state (Ahn 1994a, 1994b).

The collapsists cited economic deprivation, the apparent suspension of normal political mechanisms (such as KWP Congresses, Central Committee meetings, and Supreme People's Assembly [SPA] meetings), the failure of Kim Jong-il to assume his father's titles of president of state and secretary general of the KWP,[14] the absence of mass rallies, and elite defections, most prominently of former KWP Central Committee member and Chairman of the SPA Hwang Jang-yop, as indicators of a fundamentally dysfunctional polity.[15]

The collapsists' judgments were affirmed by a quantitative study by the South Korean government Research Institute for National Unification (RINU) that concluded that North Korea passed a critical limit of "regime crisis" in 1992, and if the regime did not respond to the intensifying crisis, the country would reach a regime change threshold during the 2001–08 period (RINU 1996). Another study by Bueno de Mesquita and Mo (1997), who formally modeled the process of transition by employing repeated game models calibrated to 1996, predicted on the basis of the potential power of each actor, their policy positions, and the

---

1994, 1997b, 1998a, 1998b). In contrast, Eberstadt (1997), in an article titled "Hastening Korean Reunification," expressed the view that "The cherished vision of a gradual and orderly drawing together of the two Koreas is today nothing more than a fantasy. As time goes on, North Korea will only grow economically poorer and militarily more dangerous. . .the faster that unification takes place, the better."

13. This quote is not atypical: both Eberstadt and Foster-Carter have remained quite consistent in arguing that the system dynamics of North Korea are unsustainable. See Foster-Carter (1997a, 1997b) and Eberstadt (1999).

14. After his father's death, Kim Jong-il eventually assumed the role of secretary general of the KWP. Kim Il-sung was made president in perpetuity.

15. Even before the defection of Hwang, for example, one observer wrote "There is at least the beginning of the transferring of allegiance of the elite of North Korean society away from the regime" (Maxwell 1996, 7).

salience each actor ascribed that issue (embodying, in their words, "a strong track record of predictive accuracy" [Bueno de Mesquita and Mo, p. 27]) and found that "Kim Jong-il's hold on power is tenuous" (p. 26) and that North Korea was entering "a period of significant political instability" (p. 25). Thought was given to the "warning signs" and the specific mechanisms of regime collapse (Collins 1996, Pollack and Lee 1999).

Such views were not atypical. When 48 multinational analysts were queried in a poll conducted by Lee Young-sun in 1995 about the prospects for Korean unification through a North Korean collapse and its absorption by the South, the modal response (29 percent) was that this would occur in the period 2001–05, with cumulatively 40 percent of the respondents expecting it to transpire by this time and 60 percent expecting it by 2010 (Lee 1995). A similar survey the following year undertaken by the *Joongang Ilbo* (September 22, 1996) found that 16 percent of the analysts expected North Korean collapse within five years (i.e., by 2001), while an additional 28 percent expected it to occur by 2006. Interestingly, 8 percent of the analysts responded that North Korea would collapse by 1998 or 1999, but that if it did make it through this period, it was unlikely to collapse for another 10 years. Only one of the 50 respondents doubted that North Korea would ever collapse. An informal poll of participants at a September 1997 multinational conference reached a similar conclusion: roughly one-third of the participants expected North Korea's collapse within five years, with the remainder splitting between those expecting the maintenance of a "hard" state and those anticipating significant reform (Noland 1998).[16]

Nor were these pessimistic views on North Korea's prospects limited to academic scribblers. During a US Senate Intelligence Committee hearing in December 1996, Senator John Glenn (D-OH) quoted from a May 6, 1996, report by the Defense Intelligence Agency to the committee: "The likelihood that North Korea will continue to exist in its current state 15 years from now is low-to-moderate. Unless solutions to the North's economic problems are found, the regime will not be able to survive. It will have to adapt its slide into irrelevance or collapse/implode. This has led many analysts to believe a process of political self-destruction has begun with potential for system collapse within three years" (Deutch 1996).

When asked to comment, Director of Central Intelligence John Deutch responded, "Either [North Korea] is going to . . . invade the South . . . or it will collapse internally, or implode because of incredible economic problems the country faces; or, third, it will over time lead to some peaceful

---

16. The conference participants were also asked to put probability weights on each of these outcomes. There was little consensus: the maintenance of the status quo was the only outcome that at least one respondent did not discount entirely (i.e., placed a zero probability weight on it).

resolution and reunification with the South." Deutch's personal assessment was that this uncertainty would "be resolved in the next two or three years. . . . It is not something that will go on for decades" (Deutch 1996). Even the US Ambassador to Seoul, James T. Laney, described North Korea as experiencing "irreversible economic and political decay" and that US policy was to "manag[e] the collapse of the system built by Kim Il-sung" (Laney 1995).

Senior officials in both the Kim Young-sam and Clinton administrations expected collapse, and the commitment to build two nuclear reactors in North Korea, embodied in the October 1994 Agreed Framework, was discounted on the expectation that North Korea would collapse before their construction was completed and that if completed the project would be managed by the Seoul-based government of a unified peninsula (Maxwell 1996, Green 1997, Oberdorfer 1997, Koh 1998). Even former North Korean officials got into the act when defecting Central Committee member and SPA Chairman Hwang Jang-yop forecast the imminent collapse of the North. Hwang, who seems to have trouble deciding on which side of the fence to sit, subsequently retracted his prediction.

Unsurprisingly, these views of government officials and opinion makers were reflected in the general public. A poll of the South Korean public conducted by the Federation of Korean Industries in May 1996 and summarized in Park (1997) found that nearly one-third of the public expected collapse within five years (i.e., by 2001), while cumulatively two-thirds of the respondents expected collapse within 10 years (i.e., by 2006).

Of course, the expectation of imminent collapse, while common, was not universally held, as demonstrated by the aforementioned survey results. The most prominent dissenting voice in this regard was that of former US Secretary of Defense William J. Perry. In a policy review commissioned by the Clinton administration, Perry wrote that "while logic would suggest that North Korea's evident problems would ultimately lead to regime change, there is no evidence that change is imminent" (Perry 1999). Analysts taking this contrary position invoked a variety of factors auguring against collapse. First, there is no clear mapping between economic distress and political change, and while the degree of economic distress experienced in North Korea has been great, it is not historically unique, as discussed later. Furthermore, the socialist model did deliver industrialization and development, at least in its initial stages—conventional estimates do not have per capita income in the South surpassing the North until the 1970s. So while North Korea did experience systemic macroeconomic problems at least as far back as 1990, if not earlier, this should be judged in the context of a political-economic system that had some track record of delivering the goods. Presumably this conveyed some legitimacy to the regime. Moreover, the amount of external support that would be necessary to keep North Korea on "survival rations" was (and remains) relatively small (perhaps $1 billion to $2 billion annually) and easily within the scope of its neighbors to provide—each of whom for their own reasons would prefer to forestall collapse (Noland 1997, Michell 1998).

Second, with the possible exception of the KPA, there is a complete absence of institutions capable of channeling mass discontent into effective political action. There is no Solidarity trade union as in Poland or Civic Forum as in Czechoslovakia. Indeed, there are not even alternative poles of moral authority capable of legitimating dissent such as the Roman Catholic church in the uprising against the martial law regime of Wojciech Jaruzelski in Poland or the "People's Power" revolt against the dictatorship of Ferdinand Marcos in the Philippines.

Externally, North Korea's neighbors have not provided sanctuary to anti-Kim political forces. There is no evidence of anti-Kim political organizing among the refugees in the Chinese border region, and there are no marauding guerilla insurgencies on North Korea's borders. In fact, North Korea's neighbors might be expected to actively cooperate with North Korean security services to crack down on such activity if it were to develop. Indeed, the absence of antiregime organizing, together with people voluntarily crossing back into North Korea, suggests a more complicated politics of deprivation.

North Korea has a Confucian or corporatist political culture likening the nation to a family led by a stern but loving patriarch (Cumings 1995, 1997). Such a political culture is inherently hierarchical. Some observers have argued that the Kim regime is unique, deriving its legitimacy not from conventional sources (i.e., the ability to deliver freedom and/or prosperity) but rather through political socialization emphasizing ideological devotion of religious intensity. This interpretation of the North Korean polity as a religious society may not be as far-fetched as it might at first appear. North Korea purged the last remaining references to Marxism from its constitution in 1992 (Foster-Carter 1997b) and has elevated the national ideology of *juche* or self-reliance to the status of "a quasi-religious moral system that purports to explain the purpose of life" (Barry 1996, 118). North Korean ideologues have gone beyond simple neo-Confucianism to address issues such as immortality more typically associated with systems of religious belief than political philosophy. In certain respects North Korean propaganda resembles a perverted form of Christianity, perhaps reflecting Kim Il-sung's upbringing in a Christian household and oddly paralleling some forms of Christianity-imbued corporatism, though nationalism appears to be the adhesive (Cumings 1997, Snyder 1999, Noland 2000).

The ascription of unique philosophical or religious insights to charismatic leaders is nothing new (Cohn 1970). What matters is their effective inculcation. Sociologist Han S. Park argues, "Political socialization in North Korea has consistently been designed to instill in the system of mass beliefs a culture that is often found in a sectarian and fanatic religion . . .

as in the extreme case of a religious cult, support is based on the existence of an unquestioning faith in the belief system" (Park 1998, 224–31).[17] Barry elaborates on this theme, observing, "North Korean society in many outward respects is the functional equivalent of a religion. It is built in concentric circles, from a pope (or even messiah), to disciples or high priests, to various orders and devout laity" (Barry 1996, 118). Perhaps the apposite comparators for the Kims are less V.I. Lenin and Josef Stalin or Mao Tse-tung and Deng Xiaoping than Moses and Joshua or Joseph Smith and Brigham Young, no offense intended to any party. Lest any readers think such comparisons are over the top, recall North Korean propaganda that describes Kim Jong-il "as a contemporary god," "superior to Christ in love, superior to Buddha in benevolence, superior to Confucius in virtue, and superior to Mohammed in justice," and, ultimately, "the savior of mankind."[18]

The implication of this line of reasoning is that the "religious" basis of regime legitimacy may buy it a certain margin of tolerance in terms of its apparent inability to deliver material prosperity or political freedom.[19] The problem, of course, is discerning whether this is an accurate depiction of the psyche of the North Korean masses, which, as Timur Kuran reminds us, is effectively impossible. Even Han S. Park, who takes the "spiritualist" argument the furthest, admits, "Whether or not these national aspirations are echoed by personal and individual citizens' aspirations is uncertain" (Park 1998, 225). On the one hand, the Kim regime was preceded by 35 years of Japanese emperor worship that, in turn, was imposed on top of what Park has termed "an age-old despotic culture," so perhaps North Koreans really are true believers (Park 1998, 225).[20]

---

17. See also Armstrong (1998) and Oh and Hassig (2000).

18. Once while in North Korea I had the opportunity to converse with my minder under circumstances that would not allow our conversation to be monitored. When he mentioned in passing that Kim Il-sung was God, I granted him that, but asked about Kim Jong-il. "Seventy-five percent God," came the reply.

19. Han S. Park, for instance, writes, "One has to realize that few countries in the history of mankind have collapsed simply because of the deprivation of the basic needs of the people. The linkage is warranted only under two conditions: economic problems bring about a legitimacy crisis for the regime, and the leadership is incapable of silencing voices of dissent. In North Korea, regime legitimacy has little to do with the economic situation" (Park 1998, 224). He goes on to assert that North Korea is unlikely to experience instability generated by feelings of "relative deprivation" due to the "remarkable level of equality in economic life" (Park 1998)—a dubious appraisal of the North Korean economy at the time and surely an even less accurate assessment after the introduction of economic policy changes in 2002, which appear to have had the effect of exacerbating pre-existing trends toward social differentiation (Noland 2003a). Even Park admits, however, that the regime cannot survive if it cannot continue the process of political socialization around the Kim cult and continues to deprive the populace of basic needs and rights, especially to food and life.

20. Bruce Cumings seems to think so in writing, "[F]oreign observers have gone wrong in underestimating this regime in nearly every way possible. Meanwhile, predictions based

Charles Burton, a Canadian diplomat and academic, wrote on the basis of conversations with North Koreans in Beijing that "the North Korean people see their political institutions as legitimate . . . for most North Koreans, even if they have their doubt about Kim Jong-il's rule and see him as a much weaker leader than his father, they do not believe that their Government is illegitimate. . . . While we might be inclined to wonder about the rituals of state and look askance at *Juche* ideology, as outsiders we should not be dismissive of the official ideology. It has its own logic and coherence and highly sophisticated people in North Korea take it very seriously" (Burton 2003, 3).

On the other hand, South Korean sociologist Jae Jean Suh (1997, 1998), on the basis of numerous defector testimonies, argues that the populace has never bought into the ideology to the degree that some might suppose, that the economic crisis gave rise to increased corruption on the part of government officials that undermined legitimacy, that there is a great gap between propaganda and reality, leading to a devaluation or loss of control over "national myths," and that the masses exhibit James Scott's passive noncompliance strategies and occasional overt noncompliance such as posting dissident handbills.[21] Or, as Aidan Foster-Carter observes, while one can blame deprivation on hostile foreigners, brutal police and corrupt apparatchiks are a different matter—they are the responsibility of the regime (Foster-Carter 1997b).

The attitudes of the North Korean masses probably lie somewhere between the attitudes of elites who have personally benefited from the system and managed to get themselves posted to Beijing and self-selected defectors, who are presumably drawn from the most alienated members of society and may well tell their South Korean interrogators what they think their hosts want to hear.

What emerges from this analysis is a regime that, while it has faced profound political and economic difficulties, internally possesses a monopoly on social organization combined with an astonishing capacity for coercion and that faces an external environment that, at least when it comes to the issue of regime survival, is fundamentally supportive. Despite evident political tensions, North Korea continues to receive more than $1 billion in foreign aid annually, including from the United States, and despite differences in opinions on this issue within the Bush administration, no foreign government today is committed to a policy of "regime

---

on the idea that this regime draws deeply from the well of Korean nationalism and political tradition and will therefore have staying power in the post-cold-war world have been correct. . . . How long this will last can be anybody's guess, but if Korean history is any guide, Kim Jong-il may well hand his baton to another son-king in the next century" (Cumings 1995, 62). While he is undoubtedly correct in the first part of the statement, one hopes that he is wrong with respect to the second.

21. See also Suh and Kim (1994).

change" in North Korea. Yet the Kim Jong-il regime actively portrays its largely self-created difficulties as a product of foreign hostility as a means of deflecting popular discontent. This strategy may be abetted by the "religious" nature of the regime that may convey an additional source of legitimization beyond conventional performance criteria and may have facilitated the transfer of power from Kim Il-sung to Kim Jong-il.[22]

Yet the future of the North Korean state remains very much a live issue. In June 2003 the ratings agency Standard and Poor's issued a report highlighting the ineluctable prospect of a North Korean collapse and its perilous implications for South Korea, identifying the prospective economically devastating costs of unification as a factor pushing down South Korean sovereign bond ratings.

Reviewing this literature, it is curious that given the gravity of the issue under consideration, these assessments were made without the benefit of a theory of regime change nor any empirical modeling of its drivers. In the absence of any real theory linking material deprivation to political change, much of the analysis tends toward a kind of casual economic determinism combined with possibly inappropriate projections of the Eastern European and German experiences onto the Korean milieu. Perhaps this is not surprising: Despite our lack of knowledge about the North Korean economy, in a relative sense we may know (or at least think that we know) much more about the state of the economy than other bases of regime support. To a man with a hammer every problem looks like a nail. But even allowing for this phenomenon, it is striking that no one seems to have attempted to bring to bear formal models of cross-national experiences with political change. Well, better late than never.

---

22. Han S. Park argues that one aspect of political socialization in North Korea has been "the creation of the charisma of two leaders, not one at a time but rather as an inseparably integrated whole" (Park 1998, 230). But this begs the question—what comes after Kim Jong-il? Kim Il-sung began publicly preparing Kim Jong-il for leadership at least as far back as the early 1970s—20 years before the elder Kim's eventual death. There are occasional rumors of plans to groom one son or another for leadership, but this does not appear to have progressed far. If a similar dynastic hand-off of power is to occur, it would seem that time is running out to begin promoting the prince.

2

Modeling Regime Change

So let's start with the nails. No one denies that economic prosperity has something to do with political stability, and everyone agrees that North Korea has gone through a bad patch since 1990. But what may be surprising to some readers is that the decline in the North's economy does not appear to be unique by contemporary standards. The verb "appear" is used intentionally—the quality of the data for North Korea is poor (as it is for some of the countries to which North Korea will be compared in this chapter). The South Korean central bank, the Bank of Korea (BOK), produces the most widely cited data on North Korean economic performance. The BOK is given this task because it would be responsible for monetary policy in a Korea unified under Seoul. The BOK estimate of North Korean national income is reportedly constructed by applying South Korean value-added weights to physical estimates of North Korean output derived through classified sources and methods and is reputedly subject to prerelease interagency discussion within the South Korean government. This raises a variety of concerns: that the reliance on physical indicators may augur an overemphasis on the industrial sector (where output is relatively easy to count) relative to the service sector, that prerelease discussions may imply interagency bargaining and a politicization of the estimate, and that the methods through which the figures are derived are not subject to independent verification. The use of South Korean value-added weights is surely inappropriate. It is rumored that a classified mock North Korean input-output table exists, though what role this might play in the BOK's calculations is obviously speculative. For all these reasons, outside analysts have at times questioned the reliability, if not the

Figure 2.1 North Korean GDP growth, 1990–2002

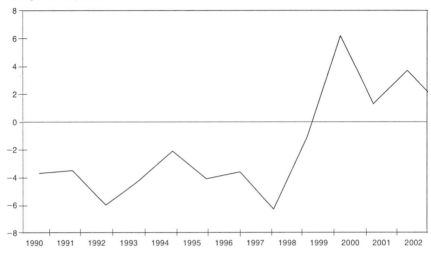

GDP growth rate (percent)

Source: Bank of Korea.

veracity, of the BOK figures (Noland 2001). Former US Vice President Walter Mondale once said that anyone who described himself or herself as an expert on North Korea was either a liar or a fool. My corollary would be to not trust any figure on North Korea that comes with a decimal point attached.

With that caveat, according to BOK figures, North Korea experienced a decline in per capita GDP of approximately 25 percent over the 12-year interval of 1990–2002, or about a 2 percent decline annually (figure 2.1). The maximum decline of roughly 33 percent (implying a compounded rate of 5 percent a year) occurred between 1990 and 1998 before the economy began to stabilize at a lower level of income. In 1997 the North Koreans themselves presented data to a visiting informational mission from the International Monetary Fund, indicating that GDP had fallen by nearly 50 percent between 1993 and 1996. There was no way to verify these figures either, however, and there was some suspicion that the decline in income had been exaggerated in a bid to obtain more aid.

Taken at face value, the BOK figures depict performance that is bad but certainly not unique by contemporary standards. According to World Bank data on national economic performance since 1960, not counting North Korea, 42 countries have suffered declines of 25 percent or more in per capita income over a 12-year period, with per capita income falling 50 percent or more in 14 of these countries (table 2.1). An examination of this list reveals certain patterns: there are no high-income countries on this list (that would be the case almost by definition), around one-third of the sample consists of postcommunist transitional countries

Table 2.1 Economic declines, 1960–2001

Country	Per capita income decline of ≥25 percent over 12 years	Per capita income decline of ≥33 percent over 8 years	Uninterrupted per capita income decline of ≥33 percent
North Korea	x	x	x
Albania	x	x	x
Angola		x	x
Armenia		x	✓
Azerbaijan			x
Bahamas		x	
Belarus			x
Brunei	x	x	
Burundi	x	x	
Cameroon	x	x	x
Central African Republic	x		
Congo, Democratic Republic of the	✓	✓	
Congo, Republic of	x		
Côte d'Ivoire	x		
Croatia			x
Cuba			x
Djibouti	x	x	x
El Salvador	x		x
Estonia	x		x
Gabon	✓	x	
Georgia	✓	✓	✓
Ghana	x		
Guyana	x		
Haiti	x		
Iran	x		x
Jamaica	x		
Kazakhstan		x	x
Kiribati	✓	✓	✓
Kuwait	✓	✓	✓
Kyrgyz Republic	x	x	✓
Latvia	x	x	x
Lebanon			x
Liberia	✓	✓	✓
Lithuania			x
Madagascar	x		
Moldova	✓	✓	✓
Mozambique			x
Nicaragua	✓	x	x
Niger	x	x	
Nigeria	x		
Peru	x		
Romania	x		x
Russian Federation	x	x	x
Rwanda	✓	✓	x
Saudi Arabia	x		x

(table continues next page)

Table 2.1 Economic declines, 1960–2001 *(continued)*

Country	Per capita income decline of ≥25 percent over 12 years	Per capita income decline of ≥33 percent over 8 years	Uninterrupted per capita income decline of ≥33 percent
Sierra Leone	✓	✓	
Suriname	x	x	x
Tajikistan	✓	✓	✓
Togo	x		
Turkmenistan	✓	✓	✓
Ukraine	✓	✓	✓
United Arab Emirates	✓	✓	
Venezuela	x		
Zambia	x		

Notes: ✓ indicates declines of more than 50 percent. General coverage is 1960–2001, though data availability varies widely. n = 178

Sources: Derived from World Bank's *World Development Indicators* unless otherwise noted. The source for North Korea is the Bank of Korea and that for Cuba and Romania is the *Penn World Tables* version 6.1.

(including former constituent parts of the Soviet Union or Yugoslavia), there are a number of oil exporters for which the precipitous declines in income were associated with movements in the world oil price, and there are a couple of countries for which the income declines appear to coincide with decolonization. Yet for the substantial number of countries that make up the remainder, there would appear to be no particular reason ex ante to expect them (as distinct from a randomly selected sample of low-income countries) to experience catastrophic declines in income. Some of these countries experienced political instability during these periods, including civil wars, transitions from authoritarianism to democracy (and the reverse), and episodes of outright state failure.

Even applying the more rigorous standard of a 33 percent fall in eight years (i.e., the worst single period of the North Korean experience), North Korea is still not alone: twelve countries suffered per capita income declines of 50 percent or more, and another 17 endured declines of 33 to 50 percent, with some countries experiencing multiple episodes of this sort. Again, about half of these cases are either postcommunist states or oil exporters, with the remainder consisting of mostly small, poor countries.

Yet another way of looking at the issue is to identify uninterrupted declines in per capita income of 33 percent or more in the data, whatever the duration of the downturn. There are 33 such episodes involving 31 countries (Kuwait and Nicaragua turned the trick twice). Around half are postcommunist transition countries, and a few more are oil exporters (although the decline in income in Iran may have as much to do with its revolution as with oil prices). Most of the remaining countries experienced civil wars or other forms of instability. This is to say that as a general proposition, uninterrupted declines of per capita income of the magnitude North Korea experienced in the 1990s do not appear to be associated with political durability.

So North Korea's economic travails are not unique, but in the face of such woeful performance is its political stability distinct? Table 2.2 summarizes data on a number of economically challenged, though long-lived, political regimes. (Not as long-lived as the Kim regime in North Korea, though. In this regard, its combination of longevity and underperformance is unparalleled.) Perhaps the closest comparator to North Korea would be Cuba, where a communist regime led by a charismatic founding leader has endured for 44 years and counting. Economic data on Cuba are available only for 1986–96, and during that period the longest economic downturn Cuba experienced was four years (1989–93) and was associated with a 28 percent decline in per capita income, actually a sharper decline than that experienced in North Korea. Small, poor, hated by the world's sole superpower, the parallels with North Korea are obvious. And as it goes without saying, Fidel Castro is still in power.

Things turned out differently in Romania under Nikolai Ceauşescu, a polity that shared a number of economic and political characteristics with North Korea, including an attempt at dynastic succession (Noland 2000, chapter 9). As in North Korea, in its initial stages, the socialist economic model delivered the goods by facilitating the mobilization of resources. But again like North Korea, Romania eventually ran into problems with raising productivity and income through "intensive" development. In the mid-1970s, after the first oil shock, both Ceauşescu and Kim borrowed money from foreign bankers seeking to recycle petrodollars. Both leaders plowed the money into dubious projects with low returns, and both countries faced a financial squeeze when the debts came due. Ceauşescu made the fateful decision to repay the loans and compressed domestic consumption in order to do so. Kim simply defaulted on the loans (the first and only communist leader to do so), understanding that if one had to disappoint a constituency, foreign bankers were a far safer choice than the local populace. The first civil unrest in Romania occurred in 1986, but it was not until 1989—with the economy in decline and revolution sweeping Eastern Europe—that protests by ethnic Hungarians in the provincial city of Timişoara metastasized into a nationwide revolt.

When it became apparent that the Soviets were unwilling to back Ceauşescu militarily, Ion Iliescu led an intraelite coup in an attempt to short-circuit the uprising and preserve the perquisites of Communist Party functionaries. The experiment with socialism in one family ended with the televised executions of Nicolai and his wife and fellow politburo member Elena. Nicu, the playboy son and heir apparent, died in exile of cirrhosis of the liver. Iliescu and the National Salvation Front were forced to acquiesce

Table 2.2 Economic downturns in selected long-lived regimes

Country	Beginning	End	Regime characteristics — Duration (years)	Cumulative per capita income growth/ decline (percent)	Annualized rate of per capita income growth/ decline (percent)	Longest downturn during the regime[a] — Duration (years)	Cumulative per capita income decline (percent)	Annualized rate of per capita income decline (percent)	Largest decline during the regime — Duration (years)	Cumulative per capita income decline (percent)	Annualized rate of per capita income decline (percent)
North Korea	1948	Present	55	n.a.	n.a.	8	-33	-5	8	-33	-5
Cuba	1959	Present	44	n.a.	n.a.	4	-28	-8	4	-28	-8
Romania	1965	1989	24	65	2	4	-3	-1	3	-7	-2
Syria	1970	Present	33	106	2	3	-11	-4	1	-12	-12
Haiti	1957	1986	29	-6	-0	2	-8	-4	2	-8	-4
Kenya	1963	2002	39	61	1	4	-7	-2	1	-8	-8
Togo	1967	Present	36	-11	-0	4	-26	-7	4	-26	-7
Zambia	1972	1991	19	-36	-2	6	-17	-3	6	-17	-3

n.a. = not available

a. In case of a tie for the longest downturn during a regime, the downturn of largest magnitude is reported.

Notes: Economic data on North Korea are limited to 1990–2002.
Data on Cuba are limited to 1985–96. Figures are reported for within this period only and are based on chained real GDP per capita (constant prices).
Economic data for Romania are taken from Maddison (2003).
Economic data for Syria are based on the period 1970–2002, for Haiti on 1960–86, for Kenya on 1960–2002, and for Togo on 1967–2002.

Sources: World Bank's World Development Indicators unless otherwise noted. The source for North Korea is the Bank of Korea and that for Cuba and Romania is the Penn World Tables version 6.1.

to democratic elections and were eventually removed from power. This denouement was not lost on the North Koreans.

Two contemporary polities that, like North Korea though not formally monarchies, have experienced father-son leadership transitions under less than impressive economic performances are Syria under Hafiz and Bashir al-Assad (33 years and counting) and Haiti under François and Jean-Claude Duvalier (29 years, 1957–86). Syria experienced a 12 percent fall in per capita income in 1989 and a three-year period of continuous decline (1981–84) during which per capita income fell by a cumulative 11 percent. In the midst of this downturn, Hafiz al-Assad turned his artillery on an insurrection led by the Muslim Brotherhood in the city of Hama, killing an estimated 10,000 residents. He retained power, which was successfully transferred to his son Bashir in 2000, a transition all the more remarkable in that the Assad regime is in large part based on the country's Alawite minority. Economic performance was considerably worse in Haiti—a 6 percent decline in per capita output over 26 years of Duvalier rule for which data are available—with the single worst period occurring in 1962–64 under "Papa Doc" and his paramilitary *Tontons Macoutes*. Yet he was able to successfully transfer power to his son, though "Baby Doc," beset with a declining economy, was eventually driven from office in 1986.[1]

A fourth possible comparator would be Kenya, where for 40 years between independence from colonial rule in 1963 and 2002, single-party machine rule was maintained under two leaders, Jomo Kenyatta and his successor, Daniel arap Moi. In 1970 income fell by 8 percent and during one four-year period (1990–94) income fell continuously for a cumulative decline of 7 percent, but the Kenyan African National Union (KANU) maintained an effective monopoly on political power. Another possible comparator would be Egypt, where a similar political machine, the National Democratic Party (NDP), has ruled for 49 years and counting through three leaders: Gamal Abdel al-Nasser, Anwar al-Sadat, and Hosni Mubarak, whose son Gamal is being groomed to succeed him. Different data sources report widely differing figures on economic performance, and as a consequence it is unclear whether the NDP has managed to preserve power through a major decline in per capita income or not.[2] Data problems also preclude comparison to Zaire under Mobutu Sese Seko.

---

1. In the infamous Luttwak (1979), appendix A, "Papa Doc" Duvalier is favorably contrasted with Ghana's Kwame Nkrumah as a leader who understood how to set the marginal revenue from taxation equal to the marginal cost of using the *Tontons Macoutes* to extract it.

2. The *Penn World Tables* show an 18 percent decline in real per capita GDP between 1971 and 1975. The *World Development Indicators* data indicate a decline only in 1973, and the International Monetary Fund's *International Financial Statistics* reports data "not available" for the whole period.

Yet another possible comparator where the full complement of data exists would be the small West African country of Togo, where since 1967 the diminutive sunglass-sporting strongman Étienne (Gnassingbé) Eyadéma has presided over an 11 percent cumulative fall in per capita income. The worst for Togo came in 1989–93, when per capita income fell by 26 percent. During this period Eyadéma was forced temporarily to permit a broadening of political participation, but he subsequently used the military to repress his opponents and has managed to preserve his leadership position since.

Zambian President Kenneth Kaunda proved less adept. As shown in the final entry in table 2.2, Zambia under his authoritarian leadership combined North Korea–like economic decline with a modicum of political stability. In 1972 Kaunda, who twice had been democratically elected in multiparty elections, used state of emergency provisions to ban the political opposition and initiated "one-party participatory democracy." Under his one-party rule, per capita income fell by 36 percent, including six years of consecutive decline (1981–87). The state of emergency and one-party rule lasted until 1991, when urban discontent forced the adoption of a multiparty constitution under which an election swept Kaunda from power.

What these examples demonstrate is that venality, brutality, and incompetence are not insurmountable obstacles to the retention of power and the maintenance of political stability of a sort. There is nothing automatic about regime change. In only two of these cases did regime change coincide with or follow immediately upon economic downturns, though the clustering of several of these episodes in the early 1990s perhaps facilitated greater than normal tolerance for bad outcomes since times were bad in many places—including in North Korea.

Background on Modeling

Thus tables 2.1 and 2.2 suggest opposing conclusions—namely that bad economic performance tends to be associated with political instability (table 2.1), but there are numerous examples of long-lived regimes that have survived periods of desultory performance (table 2.2). To parse these conflicting interpretations one needs a formal statistical model. And for this investigation one needs a more formal measure of political stability. This, of course, is inherently subjective: One analyst's "regime change" is another's "leadership transition."[3]

To address this issue (and provide an informal check on the robustness of the statistical results) three measures of political change are used.

---

3. See Przeworski et al. (2000, chapter 1) for discussion.

The first is "regime change" as defined in the Polity IV dataset by the REGTRANS variable, which captures political changes representing a minimum three-point change in the Polity score (Polity IV Project 2000). This three-point change standard "denotes a substantive, normative change in political authority considered sufficient to present greater opportunities for regime opponents to challenge the non-institutionalized authority of the polity"(Polity IV Project 2000, 27).[4] The Polity IV data for 1960–2001 cover most countries.

The second source of data on regime change comes from a change in the "type of regime" variable in the World Bank's widely used Global Development Network (GDN) Growth Database (Easterly and Sewadeh 2002), which in turn originates from the Arthur S. Banks Cross National Time-Series Data Archive maintained at Rutgers University. This dataset, while having extensive country coverage, only covers the period 1961–88, hence does not include the regime transitions in the formerly socialist states of Eastern Europe.

Finally, a third dataset was compiled consisting of countries whose per capita income declined between 1990 and 2002 by a percentage equal to or greater than that of North Korea. Excluding the oil exporters and the former Soviet and Yugoslav republics for which time-series data are unavailable, 22 countries met this criterion during the period 1960–2001.[5] Each country's individual political histories were examined using the *Political Handbook of the World* 1997 and the 2003 *CIA World Fact Book,* and significant qualitative change in the form of government due to coup d'état, democratic transition, installation of a dictator, etc. were documented. For purposes of discussion the three political change datasets derived from the three sources will be referred to as the Polity IV, GDN, and extreme-case datasets.

Each has unique strengths and weaknesses. The Polity IV dataset is the most comprehensive (essentially encompassing the entire universe of countries). Due to its larger sample size and greater dispersion of associated sample values, one might expect it to generate the "strongest" statistical results. However, if the underlying statistical relationships contain significant nonlinearities or threshold effects not adequately captured by the estimated models, the application of the model to North Korea may be misleading—that is, the model may do an adequate job of capturing

---

4. In this application, if the value corresponding to "state failure" is entered for multiple years, it is treated as a regime change in the first year only. Subsequent years of state failure are then treated as censored in the analysis.

5. The base sample consists of 27 countries. Five were excluded due to missing data. They are North Korea, the Democratic Republic of the Congo, Kiribati, Liberia, and Suriname. The remaining countries included in the sample are Albania, Burundi, Cameroon, Chad, Djibouti, El Salvador, Gabon, Ghana, Guyana, Haiti, Côte d'Ivoire, Jamaica, Madagascar, Nicaragua, Niger, Nigeria, Peru, Romania, Rwanda, Sierra Leone, Togo, and Zambia.

political change in a typical country but do a poor job when applied to the admittedly unusual case of North Korea. Conversely, the extreme-case dataset perhaps focuses the comparison on the most relevant comparators, but given the relatively small size and the fact that the sample is in effect being drawn from the tail of the distribution, the statistical results would be expected to be the "weakest": the sample size is the smallest, it exhibits the least sample variation, and the data itself are probably the noisiest, characterized by the most measurement error.

When modeling political stability there are at least two ways to formulate the analysis. The first would be to make a political regime the unit of analysis, its duration the object of analysis, and the forces that affect its duration the subject of investigation. An alternative approach would be to ask what the probability of political change is at any given point in time? In this formulation, the unit of analysis is the national polity, the object of analysis is a binary variable of whether or not this polity experienced political change in this time period, and the forces that would give rise to political change at that point in time would be the subject of investigation. The two regression metrics—accelerated failure time (AFT) and proportional hazard (PH)—produce coefficients that have opposing sign interpretations with respect to political stability; the PH coefficients represent the impact of a covariate on the "hazard of failure," while the AFT coefficients report the effect on the "expected duration."[6]

As there are multiple ways to conceptualize these models, there are multiple ways of estimating them econometrically. The basic issue is how much flexibility the functional form of the regression should be allowed to take, for example, how much a priori restriction should be imposed on the time pattern of the impact of an explanatory variable on political stability—linear, exponential, monotonic, nonmonotonic, to cite a few. In principle, one would want the most flexible, least restrictive functional form supportable by the data. All the models were initially estimated as gamma models that permit nonmonotonic duration dependence, and in cases where the hypothesis that the relationship took the form of the simpler, monotonic Weibull function could not be rejected, it is those more robust estimates that are reported.[7]

The next task is to identify the set of variables to be used as explanators of political stability. As intimated in the previous chapter, there is a large

---

6. For a highly informative introduction to these (and related) models, see Van den Berg (2000). Box-Steffensmeier and Jones (1997), Bennett (1999), and Box-Steffensmeier and Zorn (2001) review applications in political science.

7. Weibull models permit monotonic duration dependence of a positive (i.e., the hazard rate increases over time), negative (the hazard rate decreases over time), or constant (the hazard rate is time invariant) form. Only in the case of regression 3.6, based on the extreme-case data, could the hypothesis of constant duration dependence be rejected.

body of work on theories of political change and its determinants. Some of these theories are more amenable to modeling than others (in particular theories that focus on country or regime characteristics as opposed to those that emphasize its relation to the world system), and even among explanations centering on internal characteristics, there are issues of data availability, at least at the cross-national level. For example, many commentators emphasize the role of worsening income or wealth distribution or perceptions of relative depravation in political motivation (e.g., Gurr 1970). However, historical cross-country comparable income distribution data are not widely available, and data on wealth distribution or subjective appraisals of relative deprivation even less so, and what research does exist on this fragmentary data does not yield robust conclusions.[8] Similarly, if patronage is important to preserving stability, then one would want data on key constituencies and their interests. Although it is possible to think of some proxies that might be available (the military expenditure share of GDP, for example), in general it is unlikely that one can put together these data on a consistent historical basis for many countries.

As a consequence, a researcher attempting to do cross-country modeling of political change more closely resembles the drunk who looks for his lost car keys under the streetlamp because that's where the light is than Willie Sutton who according to legend said he robbed banks "because that's where the money is." (Actually, he robbed banks because it was fun and he enjoyed it.) In a statistical sense, looking for the keys under the lights has some real interpretive implications—the omission of relevant factors from the model, if statistically correlated with the included explanators, leads to what statisticians call "omitted variable bias," which may result in misleading inferences about the impact of the included variables. Under such circumstances, this sort of cross-country modeling is admittedly ambitious, if not quixotic. Nevertheless, with so much analysis of North Korea treating it as utterly historically unique, some attempt to systematically derive insights from experiences elsewhere might be considered a beneficial corrective, or at least of interest.

So where to start? Well, there is a consensus that political stability has something to do with economic performance. Performance can be summarized by *the level of per capita income* (measured either as the level itself or a *World Bank classification of groups by income level*) and the *growth of per capita income*. (Variables that were used in the regression analysis are italicized.) It may also be related to the length or *duration of economic downturns* or the *depth of economic downturns*. Other indicators of macroeconomic stability such as *inflation, the size of government, openness to*

---

8. The causal relationship between economic inequality and social and political instability is not well understood. See Perotti (1996), Forbes (2000), Przeworski et al. (2000), and the sources cited therein.

international trade, trade taxes as a share of tax revenue, and *risk of external trade shocks* may convey information about economic performance beyond the simple GDP-based measures. There is also some evidence that, ceteris paribus, being *landlocked* impedes economic performance and through this channel might have some derivative impact on political stability.

Economic performance is clearly not the whole story, though. If one thinks about the obstacles to or the "transactions costs" of organizing an insurgency, one can think of a number of country characteristics that might facilitate or impede organizing by potential contenders for power. Large countries (as measured by *population* or *area*) may be difficult to organize; high *population density* or *urbanization* may facilitate organizing. Rapid *population growth* or *growth in urbanization* may also be amenable to organizing by contributing to a growing pool of disaffected young people or new urban residents with less of a stake in the status quo. The impact of ethnic or religious diversity (measured by the *degree of ethnic fractionalization* and the *degree of religious fractionalization*) is ambiguous: on the one hand, such organizing may be more difficult in such societies, on the other, competition between rival groups may encourage mobilization. Existing evidence on the relationship between political instability and ethnic or religious heterogeneity is ambiguous.[9]

Rival groups may be further encouraged to compete over spoils if the national economy is in significant part a rentier economy based on extractive industries, though again the evidence on this is mixed.[10] The "greed" hypothesis can be investigated using *fuels as a share of exports, ores or metals as a share of exports,* or a dummy variable for a more than 50 percent *concentration of exports in a single product category* as proxies.

Political structure and heritage may also shape such competition. Daron Acemoglu, James A. Robinson, and Simon Johnson (2001) in an influential paper argued that the quality of contemporary political institutions is highly correlated with colonial settler death rates between the 17th and 19th centuries. Societies where settlers had low death rates more successfully transplanted political institutions from Western Europe than those where disease impeded the establishment of significant settler populations with a stake in local governance. Settler death rates are not available for a large number of countries (and, in any event, not all countries were colonized by Western Europeans!), but this interaction of history and environment can be proxied by *latitude* or a dummy variable for *tropical climate.* It might also be the case that differing colonial powers conveyed political institutions of differing strengths to their colonies, though previous research does not appear to bear out this hypothesis (Przeworski et al.

---

9. For various perspectives, see Easterly and Levine (1997), Przeworski et al. (2000), Arnett (2001), Alesina et al. (2002), and Collier and Hoeffler (2002).

10. Compare and contrast Collier and Hoeffler (2002), Elbadawi and Sambanis (2002), and Hegre (2003).

2000). A related argument is that a country's legal system may affect the quality of governance, economic performance, and/or political stability, with the origin of the legal system (*British, French, German,* or *Scandinavian*), whether it is a civil or common law system, and whether it originated in the country or was a transplant being among the contested hypotheses.[11]

National political history—measured as the *duration of the previous political cycle, the recentness of regime change,* and *the number of prior regime changes during the course of the sample period,* or *an index of political instability at the beginning of the sample period*—may have a role to play as well. This may either be due to a kind of simple path dependency—some countries are just prone to instability—or it may be that instability affects factor accumulation and economic performance leading to "poverty traps," though if this were the relevant channel, it might well be captured by the direct economic performance measures (Alesina et al. 1996).

It may be that external political environment conditions play a role as well—waves of democratization or waves of authoritarianism are sometimes hypothesized, but prior research does not bear this out (Przeworski et al. 2000). This kind of argument might be more plausible on the regional level, where the demonstration effects are presumably more acute, and many researchers have included *regional dummy variables* defined by World Bank categories. This begs the question of what the relevant definition of "region" is, especially with respect to North Korea. Is it Asia? Northeast Asia? Or is the *socialist country* political category really the relevant comparator?

This raises yet another issue. Some previous research has used the *transitional country* category as an explanation of political instability or regime change. But this would appear to be inappropriate since the category is literally defined by countries that have experienced regime change.[12]

Results

With more than 30 potential explanatory variables in hand, the possible permutations are almost endless. Many, many regime duration and hazard of change regressions were estimated. Many of the individual variables

---

11. See LaPorta et al. (1999); Berkowitz, Pistor, and Richard (2000); Mahoney (2001); and Djankov et al. (2002).

12. Likewise there is a considerable body of research summarized in Przeworski et al. (2000) that attempts to model specific regime transitions such as from authoritarianism to democracy. But in the specific case of interest—North Korea—we are less immediately interested in whether it makes a transition from the Kim regime to non-*juche*-based authoritarianism, democracy, or unification with South Korea, which in any event appears to be too historically specific and unique for this particular literature.

were significant when entered individually or in specific combinations. Of particular note was our inability to pin down robust results for the path-dependency variables relating to the previous in-sample and presample political histories of these countries.

In the spirit of Edward E. Leamer's plea to "take the 'con' out of econometrics," an attempt to distill reasonably robust results estimated from the three datasets is displayed in table 2.3 (Leamer 1983).[13] The first four columns report estimations derived from the Polity IV dataset.[14] Because of the collinearity among the government spending, inflation, and aid series, one cannot obtain statistically significant estimates of their coefficients when they are included jointly, although they are jointly significant, and individually significant when included without the others.

The other issue is the inclusion or exclusion of the legal origins dummies. Two of the dummies (for Scandinavian and "socialist" legal origins) are significant relative to the excluded British legal origin family. The inclusion of these variables can be questioned on a couple of grounds. First, it is not clear if "socialist" describes a legal origin or rather a contemporaneous political system. (Amusingly, the World Bank data ascribe to pre-1975 Laos a "socialist" legal origin. Too bad they didn't tell the Nixon Administration—think of all the trouble that could have been avoided.) Perhaps more importantly, Daniel Berkowitz, Katharina Pistor, and Jean-Francois Richard (2000) demonstrate that whether a country was an originator of the legal system or whether it received the legal system through transplantation may be more important than the particular legal system. Implicit evidence of this can be seen in regressions 3.2 and 3.4, where the Scandinavian legal system dummy is estimated with a huge positive coefficient. The Scandinavian class is the only one that consists purely of originators and contains no transplants. And the five Scandinavian countries in the sample had no regime changes, hence the big positive coefficient.

With these caveats, the results for regressions 3.1 to 3.4 suggest that political stability is positively associated with income level and growth; positively associated with openness and negatively associated with the trade tax share; negatively associated with the size of government and inflation; positively associated with aid and negatively associated with the tropics; and as previously mentioned, positively associated with Scandinavian legal origins and negatively associated with socialist ones.

---

13. The econometrics of this exercise are, by necessity, somewhat rough-and-ready. The classical assumption of exogeneity of the right-hand side variables may be violated in some cases, and as a consequence the conventional estimates of the standard errors are likely to be biased, though no specific violations of exogeneity were encountered in the hypothesis tests. As a corrective, the computed standard errors are the "robust" White heteroskedastic-consistent estimates derived from the variance-covariance matrix.

14. The null hypothesis of a Weibull function could not be rejected when the gamma function model was estimated, and it is the Weibull regressions that are reported.

Table 2.3 **Hazard regressions** (accelerated failure time metric, robust standard errors)

Variable	Regression					
	3.1	3.2	3.3	3.4	3.5	3.6
GDP per capita*	0.11660 (1.50)	0.12698 (1.52)	0.14181 (1.86)[c]	0.14073 (1.73)[c]	0.36969 (2.26)[b]	0.79217 (3.81)[a]
GDP per capita growth*	0.05201 (2.94)[a]	0.05240 (3.08)[a]	0.05576 (2.92)[a]	0.05606 (3.06)[a]	0.10547 (4.40)[a]	0.05078 (4.03)[a]
Openness*	0.55291 (3.23)[a]	0.51773 (3.04)[a]	0.35872 (2.09)[b]	0.32259 (1.85)[c]	—	—
Government share*	−0.02733 (−0.12)	−0.04163 (−0.17)	—	—	—	0.33068 (2.29)[b]
Inflation*	—	—	−0.05705 (−1.32)	−0.05050 (−1.29)	—	—
Trade taxes share*	−0.22119 (−2.38)[b]	−0.20194 (−2.20)[b]	−0.29303 (−2.76)[a]	−0.27536 (−2.67)[a]	−0.38182 (−1.74)[c]	—
Aid per capita	0.00418 (1.34)	0.00545 (1.63)	0.00671 (1.91)[c]	0.00808 (2.06)[b]	0.00698 (1.50)	—
Urbanization	—	—	—	—	—	−0.01509 (−2.27)[b]
Tropical climate	−0.68157 (−2.54)[b]	−0.63538 (−2.41)[b]	−0.59529 (−2.53)[b]	−0.53812 (−2.19)[b]	—	—
French legal origin	—	−0.18060 (−0.66)	—	−0.16416 (−0.59)	—	—
Socialist legal origin	—	−1.30545 (−2.74)[a]	—	−1.24638 (−3.42)[a]	—	—
German legal origin	—	−0.40262 (−0.56)	—	−0.13407 (−0.21)	—	—
Scandinavian legal origin	—	14.17375 (7.65)[a]	—	12.89373 (7.37)[a]	—	—
Constant	0.70894 (0.61)	0.82347 (0.68)	1.42718 (1.35)	1.54383 (1.46)	0.89968 (0.57)	−3.00270 (−2.18)[b]
Observations	2,531	2,531	2,289	2,289	1,727	761
Chi^2 (all variables)	81.01[a]	162.09[a]	49.39[a]	97.66[a]	43.60[a]	65.16[a]

* = Variables specified in natural logarithm form.

Notes: T-values in parentheses. Superscript **a** indicates significance at the 1 percent level, **b** at the 5 percent level, and **c** at the 10 percent level

These results paint an interesting picture. The prototypical unstable regime has overreached—it is intruding into the economy through a large government that it cannot finance except through inflation. It interferes with its citizens' ability to exploit the gains from international trade by imposing trade taxes and delinking from the world economy and in doing so encourages lawlessness in forms such as smuggling and underinvoicing and by entension the delegitimization of the political regime. In Robert Skidelsky's terms it is a "revenue" economy, unable to close the "preference gap: the gap between the government's choice of output and what the population at large would choose if it had free disposal of its resources" (Skidelsky 1996, 86). Given the possible weakness of local institutions derived from a colonial past (the tropics dummy), this ambitious state-centered agenda is being implemented incompetently or inefficiently. Aid acts as regime-sustaining "walking around money," facilitating poor governance while supporting patronage. The result is poor economic performance and an increased risk of instability.

Regression 3.5 was derived from the shorter sample period, smaller country coverage GDN dataset.[15] Again, stability is positively associated with income and growth and negatively associated with trade taxes. Aid inflows per capita are statistically insignificant, but the estimated coefficient is remarkably similar to that obtained from the Polity IV dataset.

Regression 3.6 is derived from the relatively small extreme-case dataset, and the results are somewhat different. Again, in this case, the level and growth rate of per capita income are positively associated with stability. However, government size is positively associated with stability, but urbanization is negatively associated with regime duration. The latter result is as one might expect—the more urbanized the country, the lower the transaction costs associated with antigovernment political organizing. However in this model, a large government acts as a control, and presumably a patronage, mechanism. Rather than the overreaching government, the prototype here could be Huntington's highly institutionalized, power-accumulating, democratic centralism, though admittedly, few countries in the sample would actually appear to fit that mold.

The cumulative hazard functions derived from these regressions evaluated at the sample means are displayed in figure 2.2. As one can see, there are quite significant differences. Not surprisingly, the function derived from the extreme-case dataset shows the highest likelihood of regime change, with a roughly one in seven chance of regime change in the first year, rising to a 50 percent probability of regime change by year five, and continuing to increase so that over the 41-year period, 1960–2001,

---

15. This time the hazard function is relatively flat—the null hypothesis of a Weibull function can be rejected at the 10 percent level, and the null of an exponential function cannot just be rejected at that level of significance, and the gamma function model is reported.

Figure 2.2 Cumulative hazards

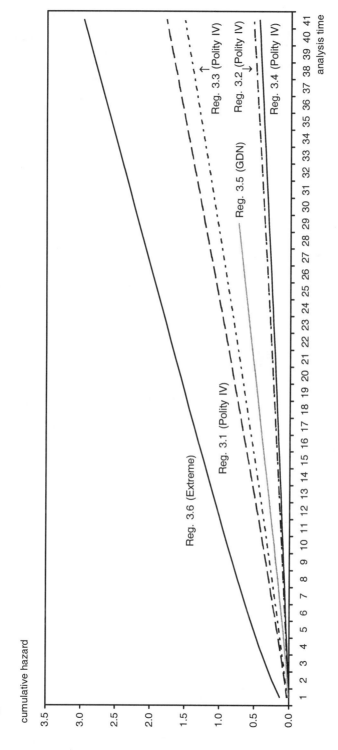

cumulative hazard

Note: Regressions 3.1 to 3.4 are based on the Polity IV dataset, regression 3.5 is based on the GDN dataset, and regression 3.6 on the extreme-case dataset.

the typical country in the extreme-case dataset would have experienced three regime changes. If this is the appropriate set of comparators for North Korea, then the country's stability is truly remarkable.

Less dramatic results are obtained from the more broadly based Polity IV- and GDN-based regressions. The cumulative hazards evaluated at the sample means derived from regressions 3.1 and 3.3 rise from less than 3 (2) percent in year one to 50 percent in year 13 (16). Inclusion of the legal origin dummies in regressions 3.2 and 3.4 depresses the cumulative hazard functions so that they rise from less than 1 percent in year one to around 50 percent in year 40. Based on these regressions, one could expect the typical country in the Polity IV dataset to experience one or two regime changes over the period 1960–2001. Regression 3.5, estimated from the GDN data, generates a cumulative hazard function that lies in between those derived from the Polity IV regressions, rising from 1 percent in year one to 50 percent in year 21.

These results refer to the underlying sample means, but we are really concerned about North Korea. To examine the North Korean case, data were constructed using BOK's income and growth data, and the remainder were derived from Noland (2000) and updated accordingly (see the appendix). Figure 2.3 displays the North Korean hazards derived from the six models. According to the Polity IV- and GDN-based regressions, the likelihood of regime change peaked in 1992 though forecast hazard rates vary enormously, ranging from 47 to 9 percent, with these differences driven largely by the inclusion or exclusion of the problematic legal origin dummies. If these variables are excluded, then the hazard rate peaked at between 9 and 13 percent in 1992 and had fallen to around 5 percent in 2002. Interestingly, 1992 was also the year that the RINU study concluded that North Korea has crossed the regime crisis threshold. As might be expected, the hazard estimates derived from the extreme-case data behave somewhat differently, peaking in 1997–98 at around 20 percent and declining to around 17 percent in 2002. Statistically speaking, those who predicted North Korea's experiencing fundamental political change during the period since 1990 were not making such a bad bet: Even in the best case, the cumulative hazard rises well above 50 percent over the course of the decade.

So much for North Korea's past, what about its future? Under one scenario, which might be labeled "cooperative engagement," diplomatic tensions are eased. North Korea receives higher levels of aid from South Korea, China, the United States, and other countries as compared to the status quo. It normalizes diplomatic relations with Japan and begins to receive postcolonial claim settlement payments. It joins the multilateral development banks and begins receiving aid from them as well. Total aid reaches $3 billion annually. Under the less threatening environment, it liberalizes its economy. The share of trade in national income rises to 71 percent, what it would exhibit if it were as integrated into the world

Figure 2.3 Hazard of regime change, 1990–2002

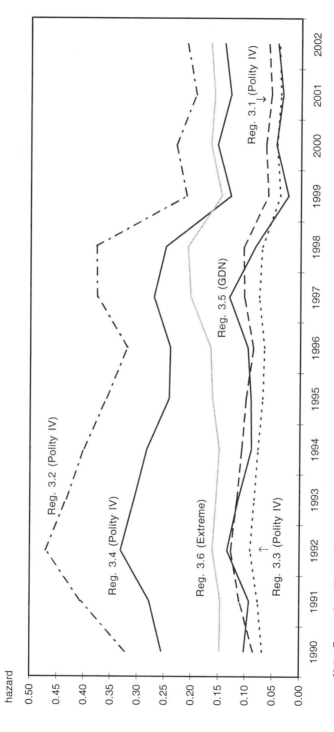

hazard

Reg. 3.2 (Polity IV)

Reg. 3.4 (Polity IV)

Reg. 3.6 (Extreme)

Reg. 3.5 (GDN)

Reg. 3.1 (Polity IV)

Reg. 3.3 (Polity IV)

Note: Regressions 3.1 to 3.4 are based on the Polity IV dataset, regression 3.5 is based on the GDN dataset, and regression 3.6 on the extreme-case dataset.

Figure 2.4   Hazard of regime change under three scenarios, 1990–2003

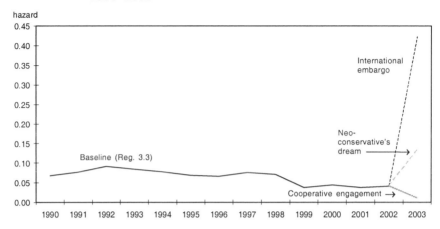

economy as a "normal" country with its characteristics (Noland 2000, table 7.2) and if trade taxes were cut to the South Korean level. The rate of economic growth rebounds to its 1999 peak of 6 percent. All other variables stay at their 2002 values.

In the "neo-conservative's dream" scenario, the global community puts the squeeze on the Kim Jong-il regime. Aid is cut off. Growth falls to its previous low of –6 percent. The inexpertly enacted July 2002 economic policy changes drive inflation up to 300 percent, reputedly its rate over the course of the year since the introduction of the reforms.

In the "international embargo" scenario, North Korea's relations with the rest of the world deteriorate precipitously, perhaps under suspicion of exportation of nuclear weapons or materials, and all international trade is cut off. Admittedly, this scenario is a stretch for the underlying statistical model, which does not distinguish between food, oil, and video games for the maintenance of a society. Some might also object that a total embargo is politically unrealistic as well. The scenario may not be without some utility, however, revealing something about the nature of regime dynamics, at least as derived from the historical record embodied in the cross-country sample.

To illustrate how these alternative developments might impact expected regime stability, the alternative scenarios are plotted in figure 2.4 using regression 3.3 to generate the predicted hazard rates. For heuristic purposes, the alternatives are appended to the graph as "2003," although there is nothing unique in the scenarios to link them to that date, and indeed, some of the changes envisioned in the "cooperative engagement" scenario would probably take more than one year to realize. Nevertheless, the simulations may be revealing in terms of how outside forces might impact regime survival in North Korea.

According to these results, under the "cooperative engagement" scenario, the likelihood of regime change falls to less than 1 percent. Kim Jong-il dies in his sleep, and one of his sons dons his crown. In the "neo-conservative's dream" the likelihood of regime change rises to about a one in seven probability, growing thereafter, and in all probability, Kim Jong-il is out of power before George W. Bush. (Remember, in neo-conservative dreams George W. Bush is in power until 2008.) In the final scenario, "international embargo," the likelihood of regime change is over 40 percent in the first year, and the Kim Jong-il regime probably collapses within two years. Gary Hufbauer, Jeffrey Schott, and Kimberly Elliott (1990) find that sanctions aimed at destabilization succeed about half the time. In comparing the results obtained in this simulation and the historical track record, it should be kept in mind that the scenario modeled involves a successful complete embargo. An embargo that was less complete by design (i.e., allowing exceptions for certain categories of exchange), or less thoroughly implemented (i.e., there was cheating) would have an attenuated impact on regime stability.

These scenarios span, but do not exhaust, the possibilities. And, of course, it is possible that contrary to the statistical model, the imposition of sanctions could afford the regime an opportunity to rally popular support in the face of foreign pressure. Perhaps the most likely outcome is something more akin to muddling through, lying somewhere between "cooperative engagement" and "the neo-conservative's dream," incorporating elements of each. The question is whether there are additional, nonstatistical insights that can be brought to bear to increase our understanding of the Kim regime's longevity—and what might come next.

3

Transition Paths

The main underlying message of the statistical results reported in the previous chapter is that the survival of the Kim Jong-il regime is in no small part conditioned on its relations with the rest of the world. This chapter delves below the statistical modeling to what might emerge from the enormously different trajectories sketched out at the end of the previous chapter. One could associate "cooperative engagement" with a process of gradual economic and political integration between the North and the South. The other two scenarios ("international embargo" and "neoconservative's dream"), carrying with them vastly higher probabilities of regime change, could result in abrupt economic and political integration on the peninsula.

South Korea is key, both economically and politically. It is key economically because it is naturally the North's predominant economic partner due to shared nationality, proximity, and the economic complementarity of combining Southern technology, capital, and management with Northern resources and labor. It is also critical politically because while South Korea may act as a protector of the Kim Jong-il regime, undercutting coercive diplomacy, its very existence as a prosperous democratic state also creates a legitimacy challenge for the Kim Jong-il regime.

To return to the themes of chapter 1, let's begin with North Korea's internal politics. One can imagine a variety of scenarios under which North Korea might experience a gradual evolution toward a less totalitarian political regime, which would appear to be a prerequisite for deep integration with the South. As previously noted, Kim Jong-il himself has spoken of the "Thai model" in which he would reign but not rule. Charles Burton envisions a future in which "Kim [is] eased out slowly over time, and rather drastic revisions made to *Juche* over a number of reinterpretations" (Burton 2003, 3). This evolutionary change is possible, though perhaps unlikely.

But even if the political and ideological foundations for a less totalitarian internal polity and gradual rapprochement with the South are not intentionally constructed, it is not inconceivable that they could emerge from post-Kim internal political competition and intervention by South Korea.

Despite hagiography that elevates him to the level of a deity, Kim Jong-il is mortal. Suppose he were to die suddenly.[1] (Przeworski et al. [2000] observe that dictators are more likely than democrats to die in office, with an unusually high number of dictators dying in air incidents. Perhaps Kim Jong-il is right to take the train.) His death could well force a significant reorientation of North Korean politics that would not necessarily imply the disappearance of North Korea as a sovereign state.

If North Korea were simply a communist theocracy existing in isolation, there would be ample reason to have one's doubts about the sustainability of a *juche*-based totalitarian regime after Kim Jong-il's demise. Yet it is precisely the state's sovereignty over only half of the divided peninsula that makes the sustainability of the most obvious alternative—a post-*juche*, non-Kim regime—problematic. In contrast to other reforming communist societies in Asia, such as China and Vietnam, the divided nature of the Korean peninsula would seem to invite disadvantageous comparisons to the South and pose some very basic issues in terms of political legitimization. The Hungarian sociologist Elemér Hankiss uses the "parable of the prisoner" to describe the political-psychological coping responses of individuals in Eastern Europe under communism. While politically a prisoner is "anaesthetized with childish irresponsibility," the existence of Western Europe provided "invincible proof that life was worth living, that it was not devoid of value and meaning, that oppression, humiliating compromises, and an existence without dignity were only a transitory episode in their lives" (Hankiss 1994, 117).

Moreover the very extremity of political socialization under the current regime that would appear to lend it some additional resilience that would seem to work against establishing a sustainable alternative basis for regime legitimacy.[2] As Nicholas Eberstadt put it, "Deprived of its raison d'être, suffering from an economic crisis, and exposed to the

---

1. Constitutional succession in North Korea is unclear (and probably irrelevant). Kim Il-sung is president in perpetuity. President of the SPA Presidium Kim Yong-nam is the titular head of state for diplomatic purposes. Kim Jong-il is the chair of the National Defense Committee (NDC) as well as general secretary of the KWP. If Kim Jong-il were to die, power would probably be contested among members of his extended family and contenders emerging from the NDC and perhaps the KWP Organization and Guidance Department.

2. Foster-Carter simply dismisses the possibility out of hand: "A workable legitimation or the continued existence of a non-Kim Il-sungist North Korean state in the 1990s cannot possibly be constructed" (Foster-Carter 1994, 32). See also Foster-Carter (1997c).

unavoidable gravitational pull of the Korean example from across the demilitarized zone, such a state would have little chance for survival. Eventually according to this line of reasoning, the state would be expected to implode—very possibly sooner than later . . . it is hard to imagine any permutation of the existing parts or adjustment of policies that would permit the survival of an independent communist state in the northern portion of the Korean Peninsula" (Eberstadt 1995, 140).[3]

Setting aside the possibilities that North Koreans, unlike Hankiss's Eastern Europeans, do not see their counterparts as "the light of hope in a world of defeat and despair," or have regressed into the "catatonic indifference" of a "vegetable," Eberstadt's formulation begs the question: what if instead of gravitational pull North Korea was subject to the centrifugal force of a South Korea fearing the cost of unification? Would a South Korean government committed to shoring up a post-Kim regime be capable of doing so?

Following the collapse of a regime, three groups typically come to the fore: revolutionaries, often making nationalist appeals; political moderates (Alexander Kerensky, Lothar de Maizière, Francisco Madero, and Abolhassan Bani-Sadr in Russia, East Germany, Mexico, and Iran, respectively); and counterrevolutionaries (Victoriano Huerta, Lavr Kornilov, and Gholam Reza Azhari in Mexico, Russia, and Iran, respectively), typically from the military, often with foreign support, for whom the main political problem is to establish legitimacy. Similarly, while the perception of a foreign threat is a usual prerequisite for the seizure of power by "top-down" revolutionary modernizers (a condition that arguably exists in North Korea), what makes the prospective North Korean case so strange is that it is the radical unifiers who would play the nationalist card, while it's the moderates, counterrevolutionaries, and top-down revolutionaries who might expect and receive foreign support—from the other half of the peninsula.

From a South Korean standpoint, the rationale for an engagement policy is quite simple. Pyongyang already holds Seoul hostage with its forward-deployed artillery. The marginal increase in effective threat associated with revitalization of the North Korean economy is minimal. Ergo, it is worth engaging with the North and hoping that through a policy of engagement either Pyongyang will evolve toward a less threatening regime or engagement will undermine the ideological basis of the Kim Jong-il regime and eventually cause its collapse. Either way the military threat to Seoul is eliminated. (Parenthetically, the same cost-benefit calculus does not hold for the United States, which has strategic interests beyond the

---

3. As Kim Kyung-won (1996) plangently observed, "[S]ubstituting the strategy of opening and reform for the failed *juche* ideology would take away North Korea's raison d'etre. North Korea exists as the antithesis of South Korea; if North Korea adopts an outward looking market economy, it will inevitably appear to be a poorer, more backward shabbier version of South Korea."

Korean peninsula, and this creates the real basis for divergence in US and South Korean preferences regarding engagement with the North.)

Suppose that the South was successful in promoting evolutionary change in North Korea—either Kim Jong-il pursues a reformist path in the North or Seoul successfully props up a reformist successor regime—what does this mean for economic integration? The key characteristics of this scenario are maintenance of two independent states and a sufficient degree of convergence of economic and political practices to make the outcome plausible. Under this scenario, it is assumed that the two independent states pursue a protracted, negotiated process of increasingly deep integration. This implies avoiding a collapse in the North while generating sufficient reform in the North's economic and political system to make some degree of integration with the South sustainable.

July 2002 Reforms

Economic policy changes introduced in July 2002, involving among other things an attempt to increase the importance of material incentives, could be interpreted as the first hesitant steps in this direction.[4] The reforms could be interpreted as having four components: microeconomic policy changes, macroeconomic policy changes, special economic zones, and aid seeking. These initiatives followed moves begun in 1998 to encourage administrative decentralization (Oh 2003). A September 2003 cabinet reshuffle holds forth the promise of younger, and perhaps more technocratic, leadership.

With respect to the microeconomic reforms, in the industrial sector there is some indication that the government was attempting to adopt a dual-price strategy similar to what the Chinese have implemented in the industrial sphere.[5] In essence, the Chinese instructed their state-owned

---

4. Assessments of both the impact of the policy changes and the political motivations behind their introduction vary. See Lee (2002), Chung (2003), Frank (2003), Nam (2003), Newcombe (2003), and Oh (2003).

5. Oh (2003) disputes this notion, arguing that the aim of the policy changes was "to shift the country's economic control mechanism from one based on material balances in a traditional socialist mandatory planning system to one managed through a monetary mechanism. . . . The situation is quite different from that in China at the beginning of its reform process, where reform-minded leaders boldly argued that economic reform measures were imperatives, not policy options" (p. 72). Newcombe (2003) also emphasizes the shift from quantitative planning to a monetized economy and reports a statement by one official that could be interpreted as suggesting a more limited aim of the policy changes: "This objective (or reform) will only be achieved by removing the last 'vestiges' of the *Soviet system* from the North Korea economy" (p. 59, emphasis in original). Frank (2003) also quotes a similar denunciation of "Soviet-type" practices. These statements could be interpreted as manifestations of a North Korean attempt to justify ideologically a uniquely North Korean "third way" policy package.

enterprises to continue to fulfill the plan, but once planned production obligations were fulfilled, the enterprises were free to hire factors and produce products for sale on the open market (Lau, Qian, and Roland 2000). In other words, the plan was essentially frozen in time, and marginal growth occurred according to market dictates.

North Korean enterprises have been instructed that they are responsible for covering their own costs—that is, no more state subsidies. Managers have been authorized to make limited purchases of intermediate inputs and to make autonomous investments out of retained earnings. They are also permitted to engage in international trade. Yet it is unclear to what extent managers have been given the power to hire, fire, and promote workers, or to what extent the market will determine remuneration. There is some anecdotal evidence that faced with this dilemma, managers are creating offshoot firms to which to transfer workers, thus getting them off the payrolls for which the parent firm managers are responsible. Amid these changes, there has been no mention of the military's privileged position within the economy, and domestic propaganda continues to emphasize a "military-first" political path.

The state has administratively raised wage levels, with certain favored groups such as military personnel, party officials, scientists, and coal miners receiving supernormal increases. (For example, it has been reported that the wage increases for military personnel and miners have been on the order of 1,500 percent, those for agricultural workers may be on the order of 900 percent, but the increases for office workers and less essential employees are less.) This alteration of real wages across occupational groups could be interpreted as an attempt to enhance the role of material incentives in labor allocation.

The state continues to maintain an administered price structure, though by fiat the state prices are being brought in line with prices observed in the markets. This is problematic (as it has proven in other transitional economies): the state has told the enterprises that they must cover costs, yet it continues to administer prices, and in the absence of any formal bankruptcy or other "exit" mechanism, there is no prescribed method for enterprises that cannot cover costs to cease operations, nor in the absence of a social safety net, how workers from closed enterprises would survive (hence the dodge of setting up offshoots and telling them to sink or swim). What is likely to occur is the maintenance of operations by these enterprises supported by implicit subsidies, either through national or local government budgets or through recourse to a reconstituted banking system, which is being restructured. Indeed, the North Koreans have sent officials to China to study the Chinese banking system, which, although it may well have virtues, is also the primary mechanism through which money-losing state-owned firms are kept alive.

In the agricultural sector, the government has implemented a policy of increasing the procurement prices of grains to increase the volume of food entering the public distribution system (PDS) along with dramatically increasing the PDS prices to consumers, with the retail prices of grains rising from 40,000 to 60,000 percent in the space of six months (Noland 2003a, table 4). The increase in the procurement prices of grains was motivated in part to counter the supply response of the farmers who, in the face of derisory procurement prices, were diverting acreage away from grain to tobacco and using grain to produce liquor for sale. Comparisons to US wholesale prices (taken as a proxy for world prices) suggest that there is still considerable distortion in the relative price structure.

The maintenance of the PDS as a mechanism for distributing food is presumably an attempt to maintain the social contract that everyone will be guaranteed a minimum survival ration while narrowing the disequilibrium between the market and plan prices. Residents are still issued monthly ration cards; if they do not have sufficient funds to purchase the monthly allotment, it is automatically carried over to the next month. Wealthy households are not allowed to purchase quantities in excess of the monthly allotment through the PDS. The system is organized to prevent arbitrage in ration coupons between rich and poor households.[6]

Some have questioned the extent to which this is a real policy change and how much this is simply a ratification of system-fraying that had already occurred—there is considerable evidence that most food, for example, was already being distributed through markets, not the PDS. But this may indeed be precisely the motivation behind the increases in producer prices—with little supply entering the PDS, people increasingly obtained their food from nonstate sources, and by bringing more supply into state-controlled channels, the government can try to reduce the extent to which food is allocated purely on the basis of purchasing power. At the same time, the state may also be motivated by broader antimarket ideological considerations as discussed later. Yet another motivation may be to reduce the fiscal strain imposed by the implicit subsidy provided to urban consumers.

However, the North Koreans have not announced any mechanism for periodically adjusting prices, so in all likelihood, disequilibria, possibly severe, will develop over time. In fact, the World Food Program (WFP) reports that since the July 2002 price changes, grain prices in the farmers' markets have risen "significantly" while the PDS prices have remained largely unchanged (WFP 2003a). Anecdotal accounts suggest that as a consequence, despite the increase in procurement prices, the policy has not been successful in coaxing back domestic supply (as distinct from international aid) into the PDS. Indeed, some anecdotal reports indicate that the PDS is not operating in all areas of the country.

When China began its reforms in 1979, more than 70 percent of the

---

6. Oh (2003) claims that the rationing coupons have been abolished, and in theory, wealthy households can buy unlimited supplies through the PDS.

population was in the agricultural sector. (The same held true for Vietnam when it began reforming the following decade.) Debureaucratization of agriculture under these conditions permits rapid increases in productivity and the release of labor into the nascent nonstate-owned manufacturing sector. The key in this situation is that change is likely to produce few losers: farmers' incomes go up as the marginal and average value products in the agricultural sector increase, the incomes of those leaving the farms rise as they receive higher-wage jobs in the manufacturing sector, and urban workers in the state-owned heavy-industry sector benefit as their real wages rise as a result of lower food prices associated with expanded supply. The efficiency gains in agriculture essentially finance an economy-wide Pareto improvement (i.e., no one is made worse off). Chinese policy-makers understood this dynamic and used the dual-price system (allowing the market to surround the plan, to use a Maoist metaphor) and side payments to state-owned enterprises, their associated government ministries, and allied local politicians to suppress political opposition to the reforms. The existence of a large, labor-intensive agricultural sector is one of the few robust explanators of relative success in the transition from central planning to the market (Åslund, Boone, and Johnson 1996).

In contrast, North Korea has perhaps half that share employed in agriculture. As a consequence, the absolute magnitude of the supply response is likely to be smaller, and the population share directly benefiting from the increase in producer prices for agricultural goods is roughly half as big as in China and Vietnam. This means that reform in North Korea is less likely to be Pareto-improving than in China or Vietnam. Instead, reform in North Korea is more likely to create losers and with them the possibility of unrest.

One result of these changes has been a noticeable upsurge in small-scale retail activity, at least in Pyongyang. Whether it extends to an industrial revival more broadly is an open question, though the consensus among most outside observers is that, at this writing, marketization has not delivered as hoped. The fall 2003 harvests are predicted to be fairly large, but it is unclear how much of this is due to favorable weather, provision of fertilizer aid by South Korea, and incentive changes.

At the same time the government announced the marketization initiatives, it also announced tremendous administered increases in wages and prices. To get a grasp on the magnitude of these price changes, consider this: when China raised the grain prices at the start of its reforms in November 1979, the increase was on the order of 25 percent. In comparison, North Korea has raised the prices of corn and rice by more than 40,000 percent. In the absence of huge supply responses, the result will be an enormous jump in the price level and possibly even hyperinflation.[7]

---

7. See Frank (2003), Noland (2003a), and Oh (2003) for recitations of other, nonagricultural price increases.

Unfortunately, macroeconomic stability at the time that reforms are initiated is the second robust predictor of relative success in transition from the plan to the market (Åslund, Boone, and Johnson 1996). High rates of inflation do not portend well for North Korea.[8]

In the short run, an initial jump in the price level is usually accompanied by an increase in economic activity, as households and enterprises mistake increases in the overall price level for changes in relative prices. This is likely to be particularly acute in North Korea, where households and enterprises can be expected to be relatively naïve about market economics and where significant alterations in the structure of relative prices will be coincident with the rapid increase in the price level. So in the short run, there may be an increase in economic activity.

In the longer run, however, once households and enterprises begin to distinguish more clearly between changes in relative and absolute prices, it will become apparent that some parts of the population have experienced real increases in income and wealth while others have experienced real deteriorations. Access to foreign currency may act as insurance against inflation, and in fact, the black market value of the North Korean won has dropped steadily since the reforms were announced, with one recent report putting it at approximately 1,200 won to the dollar in April 2003.[9]

Indeed, the authorities' treatment of the external sector has been confusing. After announcing the dramatic price increases, the government maintained that it would not devalue the currency, though this would have caused a massive real appreciation that would have destroyed whatever international price competitiveness the North Korean economy has. After about two weeks the government in August 2002 announced a devaluation of the currency from 2.1 won to 150 won to the dollar, approaching the contemporaneous black market rate of around 200 won to the dollar. A second devaluation—this time to 900 won to the dollar, again approaching the black market rate—was announced in October 2003. Tariffs on consumer products such as textiles, soap, and shoes have doubled from 20 percent to 40 percent, possibly as an attempt to deal with the overvaluation of the real exchange rate and the surge of imports into the country (Oh 2003).

The government apparently continues to insist that foreign-invested enterprises pay wages in hard currencies (at wage rates that exceed those

---

8. North Korea looks better on the third robust explanator of success in the transition (Sachs 1995)—the viability of a presocialist commercial code. The commercial code of South Korea has its origins in the colonial-era Japanese commercial code that in turn was transplanted from Germany. North Korean scholars and officials at legal workshops have exhibited some familiarity with the concepts of the contemporary South Korean commercial code based on their understanding of their common presocialist legal system.

9. James Kynge and Andrew Ward, "Back to the table: Why Kim Jong-il's failing economy may be the key to halting his nuclear program," *Financial Times*, April 23, 2003.

of China and Vietnam). For a labor-abundant economy, this curious policy would seem to be the very definition of a contractionary devaluation, blunting the competitiveness-boosting impact of the devaluation by aborting the adjustment of relative labor costs while raising the domestic resource costs of imported intermediate inputs.

Make no mistake about it: With these changes, North Korea has moved from the realm of the elite to the realm of mass politics. Unlike the diplomatic initiatives of the past several years, these developments will affect the entire population, not just a few elites. Those with access to foreign exchange such as senior party officials will be relatively insulated from the effects of inflation. Agricultural workers may benefit from "automatic" pay increases as the prices of grains rise, but salaried workers without access to foreign exchange will fall behind. In other words, the process of marketization and inflation will contribute to the exacerbation of existing social differences in North Korea. The implications for "losers" could be quite severe. According to a WFP survey, most urban households are food insecure, spending more than 80 percent of their incomes on food. And while there is a consensus that marketization is a necessary component of economic revitalization, the inflationary part of the package would appear to be both unnecessary and destructive. (If one wanted to increase the relative wages of coal miners by 40 percent, one could simply give them a 40 percent raise—one does not need to increase the overall price level by a factor of 10 and the nominal wages of coal miners by a factor of 14 to effect the same real wage increase.)

So why do it? There are at least three possible explanations. The first, alluded to earlier, is the most benign: By creating inflation, the government hopes to provide a short-run kick-start to the economy, the long-run implications be damned. (From the standpoint of North Korean policy makers, Keynes' aphorism, "in the long run we are all dead" may apply with a rather short time horizon.) Given the extremely low levels of capacity utilization in the North Korean economy, this argument has a certain surface plausibility. Yet the problems of the North Korean economy run far deeper than underutilized resources. In large part the economy is geared to produce goods (televisions and radios without tuners, to cite one example, or Scud missiles, to cite another) for which there is only limited demand. Unless there is a significant reorientation in the composition of output, it is unlikely that inflation alone will generate a sizable supply response. Even agriculture is problematic in this regard: North Korean agriculture is highly dependent on industrial inputs (chemical fertilizers and agricultural chemicals, for example), and agriculture could be disrupted if the farmers find themselves getting squeezed on the input side.

A second possibility is that the inflation policy is intentional and a product of Kim Jong-il's reputed antipathy toward private economic activity beyond state control. One effect of inflation is to reduce the value of existing won holdings. (For example, if the price level increases by a factor of 10, the real value of existing won holdings is literally decimated.) Historically, state-administered inflations and their cousins, currency reforms, have been used by socialist governments to wipe out currency "overhangs" (excess monetary stock claims on goods in circulation), more specifically to target black marketers and others engaged in economic activity outside state strictures, who hold large stocks of the domestic currency. (In a currency reform, residents are literally required to turn in their existing holdings—subject to a ceiling, of course—for newly issued notes.) In July 2002 it was announced that the blue won ("foreigner's won") foreign exchange certificates would be replaced by the normal brown ("people's") won, though it is unclear if these are convertible into foreign currency. The other shoe dropped in December 2002 when the authorities announced that the circulation of US dollars was prohibited and that all residents, foreign and domestic alike, would have to turn in their dollars to be exchanged for euros, which the central bank did not have. In the case of North Korea, the episode that is now unfolding will be the fourth such one in the country's five-decade history.

In yet another wheeze to extract resources from the population, in March 2003 the government announced the issuance of "People's Life Bonds," which despite their name would seem to more closely resemble lottery tickets than bonds as conventionally understood. These instruments have a 10-year maturity, with principal repaid in annual installments beginning in year five (there does not appear to be any provision for interest payments, and no money for such payments has been budgeted). For the first two years of the program, there would be semiannual drawings (annually thereafter) with winners to receive their principal plus prizes. No information has been provided on the expected odds or prize values other than that the drawings are to be based on an "open and objective" principle. The government's announcement states, without irony, that "the bonds are backed by the full faith and credit of the North Korean government." Committees have been established in every province, city, county, institute, factory, village, and town to promote the scheme—citizens purchasing these "bonds" will be performing a "patriotic deed."[10] Both the characteristics of the instrument and the mass campaign to sell it suggest that politics, not personal finance, will be its main selling point.[11]

---

10. The discussion in Chung (2003) suggests that purchases of the bonds may be compulsory. According to another account, while purchases are not mandatory, the authorities use purchases as "a barometer of the buyers' loyalty and support for the party and the state" (ITAR-TASS, May 23, 2003. "Bonds are being issued for sale mainly to wealthy," translation by KOTRA, May 27, 2003, KOTRA–North Korea team, Lee Chang-hak. Taken from KOTRA Web site, June 6, 2003.).

11. Frank (2003) argues that the issuance of these instruments is a response to the large expansion in expenditures associated with the increased procurement price for grain, and indeed, North Korean government expenditures appeared to increase by double

According to Kim (1998), when the government has resorted to lottery-like instruments in the past to deal with monetary overhang problems, they have been unpopular.

The hypothesis has the strength of linking what appears to be a gratuitous economic policy to politics—Kim Jong-il, who ascended to power after the death of his father Kim Il-sung in 1994 and rules as general secretary of the KWP and chairman of the NDC, not only rewards favored constituencies by providing them with real income increases but by going the inflation/currency reform route also punishes his enemies. This line of reasoning is not purely speculative: It has been reported that one of the motivations behind unifying prices in the PDS and farmers' markets has been to reduce the need for consumers to visit farmers' markets and to "assist in the prevention of illegal sales activities which took place when the price in the farmers' market was much higher than the state price" ("DPR Korean Economic Reforms," *CanKor*, August 9, 2002; WFP 2003b). A number of unconfirmed reports indicate that the government has placed a price ceiling on staple goods in the farmers' markets as an anti-inflationary device.[12]

The problem with this explanation is that having gone through this experience several times in the past (including as recently as the mid-1990s [Michell 1998]), North Korean traders are not gullible: they quickly get out of won in favor of dollars, yen, and yuan. Indeed, even North Koreans working on cooperative farms reportedly prefer trinkets to the local currency as a store of value. As a consequence, these blows, aimed at traders, may fall more squarely on the North Korean masses, especially those in regions and occupations in which opportunities to obtain foreign currencies are limited.

As an economist I am trained to assume rationality, and it is only with reluctance that I propose arguments that presume ignorance. But my personal experience in China suggests one more possible explanation for the North Korean policy. Demand and supply are not quantities or

---

digits in 2003. However, the rise in outlays associated with the increase in the procurement price for grain ought to be offset by a similar increase in revenues from the expanded PDS sales.

12. Some observers have seized on a March 2003 North Korean statement that henceforth "farmers' markets" would simply be referred to as "markets," interpreting this as an implicit broadening of the policy changes. Frank (2003) contains an intriguing exegesis on the statement in which he cites North Korean interpretations of the writings of Kim Il-sung to the effect that "farmers' markets" existed in feudal times and that "markets" will come about during the socialist transition to communism when "all consumer goods are sufficiently produced and supplied by the state and when cooperative ownership is turned into all-people ownership"—that is, the North Korean statement could be interpreted as indicating progress toward socialism, not away from it. In turn, this could be regarded either as an indication of disinterest in systemic change or as an attempt to ideologically square the circle, thus justifying contemporary policy changes in terms of acceptable ideological constructs.

points—they are schedules indicating quantities as a function of prices. Market-determined prices are thus a signal of scarcity value reflecting underlying demand and supply. My conversations with Chinese officials in the early to mid-1980s, during the first stage of the marketizing reforms, however, revealed that fundamental misunderstanding of the nature of markets was widespread, especially among older officials who had spent many years in a planned economy.

The North Koreans have indicated that they are trying to unify (or at least reduce the differences between) state prices and farmers' market prices. In a press report, one unnamed official laid out the logic of the price reform: the administered price of rice would be raised to the farmers' market price, but since no one could afford rice at the market price, everyone's nominal wages would be increased commensurately. What this official did not seem to grasp was that the amount of won in circulation was instantly increased by a factor of 10 due to the wage increase, and unless there was an immediate supply response, then the government had effectively caused a 900 percent jump in the price level. And, in fact, the North Koreans have been slow to adjust the state prices in the face of the inflation that predictably materialized in the market.

Again, political considerations increase the plausibility of this argument. North Korea's decline over the past decade has apparently been accompanied by a withering of the KWP and decline in the bureaucracy's capacity to formulate policy. By all reports, a small number of senior officials are devising the economic policy changes being undertaken in North Korea. Moreover, North Korea has a political system in which the political space of discussion and dissent is highly constricted, and the penalties for being on the wrong side of a political dispute can be quite severe. So while the logic of too many won chasing too few goods would seem elementary to those of us raised in market economies, under the circumstances that exist in North Korea, the possibility that economic decisions are being made by people who do not grasp the implications of their actions (or are afraid to voice their reservations and instead engage in preference falsification if they do) should not be dismissed too hastily.

The third component of the North Korean economic policy change is the formation of various sorts of special economic zones. The first such zone was established in the Rajin-Sonbong region in the extreme northeast of the country in 1991. It has proved to be a failure for a variety of reasons including its geographic isolation, poor infrastructure, onerous rules, and interference in enterprise management by party officials. The one major investment has been the establishment of a combination hotel/casino/bank. Given the obvious scope for illicit activity associated with such a horizontally integrated endeavor, the result has been less Hong Kong than Macau North.

The 1998 agreement between North Korea and Hyundai that established the Mt. Kumgang tourism venture also provided for the establishment of an industrial park to be managed and operated by Hyundai. While the tourism project was obviously the centerpiece of the agreement, from the standpoint of revitalizing the North Korean economy, the establishment of the industrial park, which would permit South Korean small and medium-sized enterprises (SMEs) to invest in the North with Hyundai's implicit protection, was actually more important. In the long run, South Korean SMEs will be a natural source of investment and transfer of appropriate technology to the North. However, in the absence of physical or legal infrastructure, they are unlikely to invest. The Hyundai-sponsored park would in effect address both issues. (The *chaebols*, because of their size and political connections, would not be so reliant on formal rules—they could always go to the South Korean government if they encountered trouble in the North.) The subsequent signing of four economic cooperation agreements between the North and South on issues such as taxation and foreign exchange transactions could be regarded as providing the legal infrastructure for economic activity by the politically noninfluential SMEs.

The North Korean government and the South Korean firm then negotiated for 18 months over the location of the zone, with the North Koreans wanting it in Sinuiju, a city of some symbolic political importance in the northwest of the country on the Chinese border, and Hyundai wanting to locate the park in the Haeju district, more easily accessible to South Korea. In the end, it was agreed that the park would be located in Kaesong—a decision that was hailed at the time as reflecting an increased emphasis on economic rationality in North Korea.

The industrial park at Kaesong has not yet fulfilled its promise, however: Hyundai's dissolution forced the South Korean parastatal Korea Land Corporation (KOLAND) to take over the project, and the North Koreans have inexplicably failed to open the necessary transportation links to South Korea on their side of the demilitarized zone (DMZ), though negotiations with the South on this issue continue.

In September 2002, the North Korean government announced the establishment of a special administrative region (SAR) at Sinuiju. In certain respects the location of the new zone was not surprising: the North Koreans had been talking about doing something in the Sinuiju area since 1998. Yet in other respects the announcement was extraordinary. The North Koreans announced that the zone would exist completely outside North Korea's usual legal structures, that it would have its own flag and issue its own passports, and that land could be leased for 50 years. To top it off, the SAR would not be run by a North Korean but instead by a Chinese-born entrepreneur with Dutch citizenship named Yang Bin, who was promptly arrested by the Chinese authorities on tax evasion charges.[13]

---

13. Press reports subsequently first touted Park Tae-joon, former South Korean general, head of the government-owned steel company POSCO, and prime minister, and later

More important is whether the SAR will generate any spillovers. In conventional terms this will depend on whether any lessons from the Sinuiju SAR experiment are generalized to the rest of the economy. Although the immediate prospects for the SAR appear dim, the SAR might have a more subtle positive impact if internally it is regarded as giving Kim Jong-il's unimpeachable imprimatur to the reform process. Bureaucrats and factory managers who have been reluctant to get ahead of the leadership may take this as a sign that change is safe. One possible ray of hope in these events was the removal of the less than 50 percent foreign ownership ceiling in joint ventures. Ultimately, the planned industrial park at Kaesong, oriented toward South Korea, may have a bigger impact on the economy than either the Rajin-Sonbong or Sinuiju zones.

The fourth component of the economic plan consisted of passing the hat. In September 2002, during the first-ever meeting between the heads of government of Japan and North Korea, Chairman Kim managed to extract from Prime Minister Junichiro Koizumi a commitment to provide a large financial transfer to North Korea as part of the diplomatic normalization process to settle postcolonial claims, despite the shaky state of Japanese public finances.[14] Each of the leaders then expressed regrets for their countries' respective historical sins and agreed to pursue diplomatic normalization. However, Kim's bald admission that North Korean agents had indeed kidnapped 12 Japanese citizens and that most of the abductees were dead set off a political firestorm in Japan. This revelation, together with the April 2003 admission that North Korea possesses nuclear weapons in contravention to multiple international agreements, has effectively killed the diplomatic rapprochement and with it the prospects of a large capital infusion from Japan, as well as already dim prospects of admission to international financial institutions such as the World Bank and Asian Development Bank.

Eric Hotung, a Hong Kong philanthropist, as Yang's successor. If it ever gets off the ground, it should promote economic integration between North Korea and China, though one should keep in mind that China is a big place and that the most economically dynamic parts are in the southern coastal areas far from North Korea. But the North Korean economy is so far down that even integration with a comparative backwater like Dandong could be a boost.

14. Japanese officials did not deny formulas reported in the press that would put the total value of a multiyear package in the form of grants, subsidized loans, and trade credits at approximately $10 billion. This magnitude is consistent with the size of Japan's 1965 postcolonial settlement with South Korea adjusted for population, inflation, exchange rate changes, and interest forgone (Noland 2000, Manyin 2000). Japan will certainly argue that its food aid and its $1 billion contribution to the Korean Peninsula Energy Development Organization (KEDO) should be counted against this charge. Some have speculated that Japan will even try to claim credit for the costs of recapitalizing bankrupt *Chochongryun*-controlled financial institutions in Japan. In any event, such sums, properly deployed, could go a long way in restoring North Korea's creditworthiness and financing economic modernization.

In connection with these developments, rumors circulated that the North Koreans intended to establish yet another special economic zone on the east coast, to be oriented toward Japan. Discounting the failed zone at Rajin-Sonbong, this would give the North Koreans three special economic enclaves, one oriented toward South Korea, one toward China, and one toward Japan, diversifying their portfolios so to speak. Again, given the centrality of politics to North Korean thinking, they may well envision playing the three against each other. In the long run, however, it is integration with South Korea that will be critical to the development of the North Korean economy.

Gradual Integration

Momentarily setting aside doubts about the long-run viability of these policy changes, suppose they work. What is the implication for economic integration with South Korea? In a formal sense, one can imagine a series of progressively deeper steps of integration that the states could undertake. Perhaps the first, and simplest, would be the formation of a free trade area, freeing trade between the two Koreas but permitting each to restrict trade with third parties according to their own interests. This would be equivalent to the North American Free Trade Agreement (NAFTA) in which trade is unencumbered among the United States, Canada, and Mexico, but each country maintains its own trade policies with respect to nonmembers. Even this first step would appear to be far beyond anything that can be seriously expected in the near term. The next step would be the formation of a customs union that would involve applying a common policy to trade with third parties. This would be akin to the European Economic Community (EEC).

Economic union would be a deeper form of integration, permitting the free movement of factors (labor and capital) as well as goods across borders, as exists in the European Union today. A monetary union would involve the adoption of a single currency, as is in process in some EU member states today.[15] A social union would involve the adoption of common labor and social welfare policies in the two states. The final stage would be political union and the surrender of independent claims on sovereignty.

Cooperation could be expected to yield economic benefits to North Korea in the form of enhanced trade and investment, assistance from South Korea and the multilateral development banks, and settlement of postcolonial claims against Japan. For $2 billion annually, one could fix the North Korean economy sufficiently that it would generate rising living standards. (Whether this would ultimately contribute to political stability

---

15. See Park and Müller (2001) for a proposal for gradual monetary integration of North and South Korea.

is another issue, though.) Around half of this would be for recurrent flow consumption expenditures, and around half would be for industrial and infrastructural investments that could be self-financed through export revenues, so that the necessary recurrent external financing needs would be around $1 billion annually. This would be a fairly bare-bones rehabilitation effort, though: James Williams, Peter Hayes, and David Von Hippel (1999), for example, estimate that a rural energy rehabilitation program would cost about $2 billion to $3 billion over five years. Their estimated price tag for a more comprehensive economywide program is $20 billion to $50 billion over 20 years. An Iraq-like attempt to nearly instantaneously increase living standards to some happy-ending steady-state path would require Iraq-like infusions of capital.

The most obvious source of funding for revitalization would be aid from South Korea. This, of course, is nothing new—South Korea regularly provides the North with food and fertilizer worth hundreds of millions of dollars and in June 2000 the South Korean government sent $500 million to ensure the consummation of the Pyongyang summit meeting between North Korean leader Kim Jong-il and South Korean President Kim Dae-jung.[16]

The United States is another source of aid. Between 1995 and 2002 North Korea received more than $1 billion in food and energy assistance from the United States, making it in the late 1990s the largest aid recipient in Asia. Even under the George W. Bush administration, assistance has been more than $100 million annually. Presumably these figures would jump if diplomatic tensions could be resolved. Another important source of finance would be the resolution of North Korea's postcolonial claims against Japan as envisioned in the statement of Japanese Prime Minister Koizumi following his September 2002 summit meeting with Kim Jong-il.

Membership in the international financial organizations would be yet another possible source of funding. Pyongyang has periodically expressed interest in joining the International Monetary Fund (IMF), the World Bank, and the Asian Development Bank (ADB), though membership talks have never made much progress, snagging on North Korea's unwillingness to permit the kind of access to economic data and information required for membership in these organizations and diplomatic opposition relating to unresolved political issues.[17] Moreover, in the absence of considerable

---

16. In September 2003, five government officials and one Hyundai Asan executive were convicted on corruption charges associated with the June 2000 payment. Another Hyundai executive's court decision was postponed pending the outcome of another corruption trial. Hyundai Asan Chairman Chung Mong-hun, under indictment for illegally channeling money to the North, committed suicide in August 2003. There have been unproven allegations of other illicit payments to North Korea to induce participation in other bilateral meetings.

17. In the case of Japan, these concerns have revolved around the abductees issue. In the case of the United States, the US executive directors at the development banks would be

reorientation in North Korea's domestic economic policies, it would be unlikely that the multilateral development banks would make significant loans even if North Korea did become a member. Technical advice and assistance would really be more important than direct lending activities, which would ultimately only complement the activities of private investors. However, assuming that all these issues were resolved, working from the case of Vietnam (another Asian transitional economy where the government undertook rapid economic reforms) and scaling down the multilateral development banks' lending program for the smaller size of the North Korean population, one obtains lending on a scale of $150 million to $250 million annually.[18] Bank staff have also expressed the view privately that an independent, poor North Korea would probably be able to access more lending than a unified middle-income Korea.

A final source of public funding could be a revision/renegotiation/ extension of the 1994 Agreed Framework between the United States and North Korea, under which a multinational consortia, largely funded by South Korea and Japan, agreed to build the North Koreans two nuclear reactors. Given the state of North Korea's infrastructure, the investment of billions of dollars in two nuclear reactors would be daft—the reactors could not be safely operated without rehabilitating North Korea's creaky electrical power grid, and in any event, the money could be better used on alternative investments. Scrapping the costly light water reactors and instead building more cost-effective electrical generating systems, refurbishing the existing electrical grid, and building the necessary infrastructure would allow North Korea to export electricity to South Korea and China and export other products globally, thereby earning foreign exchange (Von Hippel and Hayes 1998).

At the same time, to obtain these benefits, North Korea would have to forgo its current revenues from exportation of medium-range missiles and weapons of mass destruction, drug trafficking, and counterfeiting, which may run as high as $1 billion annually. Furthermore, North Korea would have to settle private claims arising from past international loan defaults, were it to reenter international capital markets.

---

legally prohibited from voting in favor of extending loans to North Korea until it was removed from the list of countries engaging in state-sponsored terrorism. See Noland (2002a) for discussion.

18. It is possible that under some circumstances, North Korea could obtain international financial institution loans even if it were not a member. For example, the World Bank maintains a special program for peace and sustainable development in the Middle East through which it makes loans in the areas controlled by the Palestinian Authority. It also has adopted a policy that allows it to assist countries that are emerging from crises even though they are not members in good standing of the Bank. This policy was adopted after the Bank was precluded from lending to Cambodia because of a debt arrearage problem. The key attributes in these cases appear to be a cooperative recipient government and strong support from major Bank shareholders.

In sum, if there were sufficient reduction in external tensions and internal policy reform, North Korea would face a fairly supportive international environment. What might be the effect of North Korean economic reform on the North and the South?

Even in today's relatively tense diplomatic environment, North Korea's incessant claims that the United States is out to "stifle" it ring hollow, as the primary constraints on North Korean development are self-imposed.[19] North Korea is probably the world's most distorted economy. Fundamental reform would have two profound effects: First, there would be a significant increase in exposure to international trade and investment.[20] Second, changes in the composition of output could be tremendous, involving literally millions of workers changing employment (Noland 2000, chapter 7; Noland, Robinson, and Wang 2000a).[21] Both developments could be expected to have enormous political implications, and as a consequence the rapidity by which reform was introduced would be affected by the resemblance of the reform-implementing government to the regime currently in power and hence reflect existing power configurations. A transition under Kim Jong-il would presumably yield relatively hesitant piecemeal changes, while an authoritarian government that came to power after some period of political turbulence might owe less to incumbent interest groups and might have more leeway to break with the status quo. Given the extraordinary degree of militarization of North Korean society, a reduction in diplomatic tensions accompanied by a major demobilization of conventional forces would yield a large peace dividend.

From a North Korean perspective, qualitatively similar results would be obtained if it liberalized preferentially and formed a customs union with South Korea (Noland, Robinson, and Liu 1999; Noland, Robinson, and Wang 2000b). Trade with both South Korea and the rest of the world

---

19. To cite one example, North Korea chronically fails to fill its Multi-Fiber Arrangement quotas on textile and apparel exports, even in markets such as Japan and the European Union where it has never faced politically determined constraints. Indeed, it was precisely this situation that generated transshipping activity by producers from quota-constrained countries attempting to circumvent the quota constraints.

20. North Korea does encounter the problem that it does not have normal trade relations (also known as most favored nation status) in trade with the United States. As a consequence, it faces very high tariff barriers in some sectors such as apparel in which it might have comparative advantage. North Korea could establish Normal Trade Relations as part of a process of political normalization under this reform scenario.

21. Even in the case of large financial inflows from abroad, which would drive up the real exchange rate, the traded-goods sector of North Korea would expand relative to the base. The rate of return on capital would rise, as would real wages for all classes of labor, with the largest increases experienced by the highly skilled. Assuming that the highly skilled would emerge as the predominant owners of capital, these effects would imply an increase in income and wealth inequality in North Korea (though this would occur in the context of a dramatic reduction in poverty).

would increase, and, from the standpoint of the whole peninsula, the customs union would be strongly trade creating. In the customs union scenario, integration with the North would have a modest positive impact on South Korea. Trade with North Korea would mostly substitute for trade with other countries and, given the small size of North Korea relative to South Korea, trade creation and diversion would have a trivial impact on South Korea. The distributional implications would be minor, and according to the model, formation of a customs union would be Pareto-improving.

The risks for South Korea of this engagement strategy are not the ones that would create symmetric dependency as is sometimes alleged. The disparity in the relative economic impact would be reinforced by disparity in political and social impacts as well. The process of economic integration would create highly asymmetric dependency in favor of the South. The real threat to the South of economic integration lies elsewhere. The South Korean economy has real problems with nontransparent and corrupt government-business relations. In the North, there is no real difference between the state and the economy. Any large-scale economic integration between the North and the South will be by its very nature a highly politicized process and will in all likelihood retard progress in cleaning up business-government relations in the South. The corruption scandals involving the Blue House and the Korean Development Bank with respect to Hyundai Asan's activities in the North are exhibit A in this regard. This does not have to be: There are ways, through the tax code for example, to encourage South Korean economic integration with North Korea in a transparent and relatively efficient manner. Such an approach would have the added benefit of encouraging learning and adaptation to actual market-based economics in the North, while weaning it from politicized aid-seeking. But these approaches have not been tried by Seoul.

Furthermore, while the reform scenario appears relatively attainable, there is no guarantee that such an outcome will be obtained. Up to this point, the global community's approach to dealing with the North has been aid-centric in practice if not in name. A fundamental question is whether aid is likely to encourage or impede the transformation of the Kim family regime?

There is a large economic literature on the fungibility of aid, its impact on policy, and its impact on growth. The message of this literature is that aid tends to be fungible and simply supports government consumption according to the pre-existing preferences of the recipient governments. (Even in the specific case of humanitarian food aid provided in-kind to North Korea, one effect has been to crowd out food imports on commercial terms, acting as implicit balance-of-payments support [Noland 2003a].) There is also little evidence that aid buys policy reform by the recipient government, rather it may alleviate financial pressures to reform and instead weaken accountability and encourage temporizing behavior. For these reasons there is virtually no evidence to support the general proposition that aid promotes growth, and its efficacy even in countries with good policies is now in doubt (Easterly, Levine, and Roodman 2003).[22]

This reinforces the previously obtained econometric result that aid contributes to political stability independent of growth by increasing resources available for regime maintenance. In essence, aid is a pure rent to the incumbent who can dole it out with the sole object of maintaining his incumbency. Indeed, recent research suggests that aid may actually undermine the quality of governance by encouraging corruption in the public sector and diversion in the private sector of scarce human resources from productive activities into rent-seeking. Anecdotal evidence of growing social differentiation in North Korea, in part due to the misappropriation of aid for private purposes, is consistent with this view. Even in the case of in-kind humanitarian food assistance provided to North Korea, the provision of this aid conveys enormous rents, and there are widespread though admittedly unproven claims that aid shipments have been diverted into the market by rent-seeking apparatchiks.

North Korea currently receives considerable aid from South Korea, China, the United States, and other members of the international community, unconditioned on economic policy. (If there is any conditionality at all, it relates to foreign policy issues, particularly bilateral political relations between North and South Korea and the North Korean nuclear program [Noland 2000, table 5.3].) It is possible that the government of North Korea might use these capital inflows to promote economic reform. The initiation of economic policy changes in July 2002 demonstrates an intention to improve the efficiency of the economy, if not fundamentally alter its workings. Yet in terms of the structure of its economy, the relatively industrialized North Korea more closely resembles Romania, Belarus, and some other Eastern European countries than the relatively agrarian China or Vietnam at the time that they initiated their reforms (Noland 2000, table 3.7). The restructuring of industrial enterprises in North Korea is likely to create losers, at least in the short run, and as in the case of Eastern Europe, political opposition to reform. The counterargument is that the North Korean economy has sunk so far that incumbent firms, workers, and politicians will accept any reform as potentially welfare enhancing, and there is almost surely some truth to this observation. In this context, a reformist government might use aid inflows to

---

22. See, for example, Pack and Pack (1990, 1993) and associated citations on fungibility. On the apparent inability of aid to induce policy change, see Burnside and Dollar (1997) and Dollar and Svensson (2000); and on aid's potentially detrimental effects on governance, see Knack (2000) and Svensson (2000). Svensson (1999) finds that the long-run growth-promoting effect of aid is conditional on political rights. Needless to say, those are in short supply in North Korea.

pacify a potentially restive population during a painful transitional period of restructuring. So there is a case to be made that a reformist North Korean government could put aid inflows to good use.

However, such behavior, objectively speaking, would be highly unusual. Rather than using aid to ease painful transitions, most governments use aid to temporize and avoid implementing policy changes. When aid is used to support reform, it is often in the context of a new, sometimes democratic, government trying to make a break with the past, not a half-century-old regime under an incumbent leader. And it goes without saying that while the North Korean government did initiate policy changes in July 2002, they have been a mixed bag, possibly reflecting some serious misunderstandings of the workings of markets. While the government has introduced new slogans extolling efficiency improvements, it continues to proclaim "military-first" politics incessantly and has a history of hesitant and timid responses in the economic policy arena. This is simply to say that while engagement on market terms may indeed encourage learning and evolutionary change, in the specific case at hand, the odds are that the provision of aid will retard constructive change, not promote it. The result may be something closer to "muddling through" than the aggressive opening and reconciliation envisioned in "cooperative engagement."

For that matter, even the most adroitly implemented engagement policies cannot guarantee the hoped-for outcome of peaceful evolutionary change in the regime. The extraordinary politicization of life in North Korea implies that a change in political relations cannot be limited to a relatively discrete sphere—instead political change would have a comprehensive impact on virtually all aspects of social life. This condition would appear to portend difficulty in establishing a sustainable alternate polity. In short, the "cooperative engagement" scenario of the previous chapter may not be in the cards.

"Radical" Integration

Suppose that North Korea was not able to manage a gradual political transition successfully. Although North Korea today does not appear to embody the characteristics of a prerevolutionary society, nonrevolutionary transitions out of communism are problematic, and the divided-nation aspect of the Korean peninsula presumably would create difficult legitimization issues for any post-*juche* regime. The "collapsists" may not be alone in their unfulfilled dreams: the expectation that the two parts of the Korean peninsula will unify through a gradual, consensual, and protracted process of integration lasting generations, the official position of both Korean governments, would appear to be in large part based on wishful thinking.

The most likely outcome of an abrupt political transition in North Korea would be its eventual absorption into South Korea and its disappearance as an independent state. This is not the only possible outcome, to be sure. The most frightening possibilities would include a forcible unification attempt or a civil war in which one or more factions appealed for external assistance, potentially drawing South Korea, the United States, and China into military activities. Nevertheless, the peaceful collapse and absorption scenario is useful for illustrating some alternative conceptions of the economic precursors to unification as well as to its effects—even if continued muddling through under Kim Jong-il or some successor is a more likely outcome.

The relatively cheap gradual reform scenario depends on the stability of the North Korean state and the consequent ability to maintain enormously different levels of income across the two parts of the Korean peninsula. Specifically it depends on factor markets in the two parts of the peninsula not being allowed to integrate. A collapse would set in motion economic and political forces that would make the maintenance of such enormous disparities difficult, if not impossible, to sustain for any protracted period of time.

On the basic comparisons, the prospective Korean case does look worse than the case of Germany to which it is usually compared: In relation to South Korea, North Korea is larger and poorer than East Germany was in comparison with West Germany. The one criterion in which the Korean case comes out ahead is demographics: North Korea has a younger population than East Germany and young North Koreans are presumably more risk-taking and adaptable than middle-aged East Germans. Moreover, with a younger population, the existing educational and training institutions can play a central role in preparing the new democratic, market-oriented society.

Yet the relatively larger, poorer, and younger population of North Korea all points to migration as being a potentially more important issue in the Korean case than in the German case. The government would face rising expectations among the populace of the North and a desire to migrate south in search of better lives. It is possible, though unlikely, that the government could use the DMZ as a method of population influx control for an extended period of time while conditions in the North slowly improved. Rather, the political imperative would be to improve conditions in the North rapidly.

The conventional wisdom that the fundamental German policy error was in overvaluing the East German mark at the time of monetary union is wrong and obscures more important lessons of how to manage institutions during a transition. A more careful analysis suggests that it was wage policies—a product of German institutions and political incentives—not the exchange rate that priced East German labor out of the market. Moreover, misguided labor-market policies were compounded by mistakes regarding privatization and restitution policies, as well as competition (antitrust) policies, all of which combined to greatly reduce the demand for goods produced in East Germany.[23] However, even under a relatively optimistic scenario of moderate, controlled, cross-border migration, and rapid convergence in North Korea toward South Korean levels of productivity, bringing the level of income in North Korea to half that of the South would require a decade and hundreds of billions of dollars of investment—and, contingent on the amount of investment that could be financed from abroad, internal transfers similar in relative magnitude to the German case (Noland, Robinson, and Liu 1998; Noland, Robinson, and Wang 2000b; Funke and Strulik 2002). Of course the status quo already embodies transfers—South Korea is providing North Korea with hundreds of millions of dollars annually; the difference is that this assistance is provided unconditionally and presumably used for regime maintenance and not social welfare.

A key variable affecting virtually every issue of interest would be the magnitude of cross-border labor migration from the North to the South. Migration would act as a substitute for capital transfer. The more labor were allowed to migrate, the lower the amount of capital investment necessary to reconstruct the North Korean economy. If no investment were undertaken and North Koreans were able to freely move south, North Korea would be virtually depopulated before differences in income levels were sufficiently narrowed to choke off the incentive to migrate. Conversely, if incomes in North Korea were raised solely by infusions of capital investment, the amount needed to choke off the incentive to migrate could be as high as $1 trillion, out of reach of the South Korean taxpayer. Presumably, neither of these outcomes is acceptable to South Korea, so the real issue is the form of an intermediate solution that would involve a combination of cross-border movements in both labor and capital.

Several key factors will determine the macroeconomic impact on the South Korean economy of a collapse and absorption of North Korea along the lines of the German experience:

- What efficiency gains are possible in North Korea simply through marketization and the removal of self-imposed distortions—without any additional resources?

- How fast can North Korea absorb new technology?

- How much labor will be permitted to migrate from the North to the South?

---

23. See Sinn and Sinn (1996), Watrin (1998), Wolf (1998), Noland (2000, chapter 8), and references therein for more extensive discussions of the German "lessons" for Korea.

- How much capital will be invested in the North? How much will come from the South and how much from other parties? Will this capital be invested on market or concessional terms?

Depending on how these factors are parameterized, one can come to a variety of conclusions about the impact of collapse on the South. Choosing a plausible and prudent set of parameters, the models suggest that over the course of a decade, the collapse and absorption scenario would yield the following results:

- A mild slowing of the South Korean growth rate, a rapid acceleration of the North Korean growth rate, and an increase in peninsular output relative to the no-collapse scenario (Noland, Robinson, and Wang 2000b; Funke and Strulik 2002).

- Within South Korea a shifting of income from labor to capital, and within labor, from relatively low-skilled to relatively high-skilled labor. If one assumes that capital is predominantly owned by high-skilled labor, then this suggests that the process will be accompanied by increased income and wealth inequality in South Korea (Noland, Robinson, and Liu 1998; Noland, Robinson, and Wang 2000b).

- Across the various sectors of the South Korean economy, there would be a tendency for sectors such as construction to expand, while the internationally traded goods sectors would be disadvantaged (Noland, Robinson, and Liu 1998; Noland, Robinson, and Wang 2000b).

- There would be a modest peace dividend in the South and a huge peace dividend in the North (Noland, Robinson, and Wang 2000b).

In sum, while collapse and absorption would negatively impact the South relative to a no-collapse scenario, the effect is relatively modest, and a South Korean government committed to cushioning the impact on the poorest parts of South Korean society could do so through the adoption of appropriate policies.

Put crudely, in the collapse and absorption scenario, the economics come down to the movement of Southern money north or the movement of Northerners south. The policies that are ultimately adopted will be a function of politics. A number of cleavages are possible: between the North and the South, and within South Korea between capital and labor (owners of capital viewing Northerners as a new source of cheap labor, and labor regarding the North as a potential source of labor-market competition). Cleavages within the South Korean labor force, between high-skilled and low-skilled workers, could also occur. Depending on the macroeconomic policies applied, the internationally traded and nontraded goods sectors could be affected in very different ways, opening up another cleavage.

In the event of collapse and absorption, a whole host of unification issues (conversion rate of North Korean won to South Korean won, assignment of property rights, etc.) have enormous implications for the economic welfare of current residents of North Korea. The extent to which they are afforded a voice in politics will be a critical aspect of the unification process. Effective participation by Northerners would appear to rule out some policies, such as proposals to maintain the DMZ and administer North Korea as a special administrative zone, which would prevent the equilibration of wages and rates of return on capital between the North and the South, or proposals for the South Korean government to retain rights to all assets in the North.[24] Conversely, policies that would deny to Northerners gains from the unification process would only be sustainable if their participation in democratic politics were circumscribed. Thus a key economic issue is the extent to which the North Koreans would be full participants in the political system of a unified Korea.

The question then arises: What, if anything, can South Korea, the United States, and others do to prepare for such a contingency? South Korea's need to prepare for the contingencies of unification with North Korea and its need to strengthen its financial system in the wake of its own financial crisis coincide. In the event of unification, there is absolutely no reason to finance the construction of infrastructure out of current tax receipts. Instead, the government will want to use both taxes and bonds to finance unification expenditures. Hence the development of a robust government bond market prior to unification should be a priority. A second consideration runs in the opposite direction: having surmounted the 1997–98 financial crisis, South Korea will want to return to a policy of fiscal rectitude and salt away some reserves for this potential rainy day. A strong government financial position would both allow it scope for immediate expenditures in the event as well as facilitate the issuance of "unification bonds." As a consequence, the South Korean government needs to develop benchmark bonds, even if they are unnecessary, strictly speaking. Some observers have ascribed current Korea Development Bank borrowing in international markets to this motivation.

At the moment of collapse in this scenario, there will be a critical need for close coordination among the militaries of the United States, South Korea, and China, since presumably they will be central to maintaining order, handling refugee flows, etc. This cannot be overemphasized, though further discussion is really beyond the scope of this policy analysis. Once the situation on the ground has stabilized, longer-run political and economic policies come to the fore. As indicated earlier, there is an extensive literature on the lessons for Korea from German unification, and the South Korean government has devoted considerable resources to studying this topic.

---

24. See Young, Lee, and Zang (1998) for a proposal along these lines.

At the time of unification, the South Korean government will have multiple (and potentially conflicting) policy objectives. On the one hand, maintenance of economic activity in the North on market-consistent terms will be the top priority. At the same time, the government should seek to effect a one-time-only wealth transfer to the current North Korean population since they will have to adjust to market institutions with virtually no household wealth. One can imagine a multipronged approach:

- Adopt dual-rate monetary conversion. Aim for slight undervaluation of the North Korean won to maintain competitiveness, thereby making North Korea an attractive location for investment. Convert personal saving at an overvalued rate (effecting a wealth transfer).

- Deed land to the tiller and the housing stock to its occupants, contingent on maintained use for some specified period of time.

- Maintain some kind of temporary, emergency, nonmarket social safety net in the North.[25]

Having given the land to the tiller, one must confront the issue of property rights claims by past owners or their descendants and the more general issue of assignment of property rights to commercial or industrial assets. Lessons learned from the experience of Germany and other former centrally planned economies (CPEs) are instructive in this regard:

- Avoid the policy of restitution for seized assets. Monetary compensation for seized assets might be considered, though even some South Korean analysts have argued that this would be a mistake.

- Privatize quickly and avoid the cash-on-the-barrelhead model. Abolish interenterprise debts.

- Emphasize investment, not consumption, transfers.

- Accept assistance from foreigners, including the Japanese.

With respect to privatization, the experience of East Germany and other CPEs suggests that it would be best to move quickly and avoid the cash-in-advance model, since it would severely restrict potential buyers. Attempts to restructure these enterprises before privatization should also be avoided. That is better left to the market. Interfirm debts, which are a legacy of irrational policies under the centrally planned regime, should be written off. Debt-equity swaps could be used to pay off external debt and at the same time create stakes in the viability of North Korean enterprises for South Korean or foreign firms.

---

25. These policy recommendations are discussed in greater detail in Noland (2000).

Given these considerations, there appears to be one institution in South Korea ideally suited for the task of making North Korea competitive: the *chaebol*. Unfortunately, one policy goal (to get the North Korean economy functioning as rapidly as possible) and another policy goal (to clean up business-government relations in South Korea) would conflict. It goes without saying which one will receive the greater weight. The *chaebol* are probably ideally suited for refurbishing the North Korean economy. However, saddling them with unproductive North Korean enterprises would have an economic price (in terms of reducing *chaebol* competitiveness internationally and possibly encouraging anticompetitive behavior domestically) as well as a political one (in the form of the quid pro quos that the *chaebol* could be expected to extract).

With respect to the other actors, many of the policies that one would want to see in place in the case of collapse (North Korean involvement with the international financial institutions, for example) are really not contingent on collapse. Since in the case of collapse one would want to see the multilateral development banks involved as quickly as possible, it would make sense to get them involved and develop some country-specific knowledge and expertise prior to the event.

A big money issue in any scenario will be how to settle postcolonial claims against Japan, which could involve financial transfers on the order of $10 billion. If this were not done before collapse, it would be essential that Japan and the government of Korea quickly reach an accord so that funds could begin flowing as soon as possible.

4

Implications for South Korea

For better or worse, the futures of North and South Korea are inextricably bound together. This linkage raises profound questions about the capacity of South Korea's still-maturing democratic political culture and about the economic and political issues posed by its relationship with the North and derivatively with other countries, most importantly the United States, China, and Japan. As much as the economic "miracle on the Han" is a well-deserved source of pride, it is the political evolution of the South—from military authoritarianism to managed elections to truly contested elections and empowerment of a once despised political opposition in little more than a decade—that is an even more compelling legacy.

The most difficult political issues would be created by the collapse and absorption scenario and the requirement to somehow give voice to the current residents of North Korea and incorporate them into South Korea's political culture. Presumably this would be accompanied by some kind of "lustration policy" to ban high-ranking members of the Kim Jong-il regime from holding positions of responsibility in a democratic unified Korea. Yet even the less apocalyptic scenarios of gradual integration pose their own challenges. How does a democratic polity like South Korea accommodate itself to the antithetical values represented by the North's dynastic Stalinism? Would the exigencies of engagement reflect themselves in the corruption and stifling of civil liberties as observed over the past several years? (Though to be fair, this cannot be blamed entirely on the engagement with the North—corruption and stifling of civil liberties seem to be regrettably enduring features of South Korean political culture.) How can South Korea's political leadership create a national consensus—so evidently absent today—on how to handle the North?

Likewise, while a collapse of North Korea could create dangerous international situations of great immediacy—possibly involving military forces from South Korea, the United States, China, and Japan—the more prosaic process of gradual rapprochement between Pyongyang and Seoul carries with it its own burdens. The most obvious is in terms of South Korea's relations with its alliance partner and security guarantor, the United States. Today, increasing numbers of South Koreans, accustomed to living for decades in the shadows of the North's forward-deployed artillery, do not regard the North as a serious threat. Growing prosperity and confidence in the South, in marked contrast to the North's isolation and penury, have transformed fear and loathing into pity and forbearance. Instead, it is the United States, an ocean away, that regards the North and its nuclear weapons program with alarm. As the United States has focused on the nuclear program, its ally, South Korea, has observed the North Koreans' nascent economic reforms and heard their talk of conventional forces reduction, and the gap in the two countries' respective assessments of the North Korean threat has patently widened. The divergence in threat perceptions has been reinforced by differences in attitudes toward a host of bilateral and global issues that have emerged in the post–9/11 world. (The Pew Research Center for People and the Press survey "What the World Thinks in 2002," for example, revealed that of 27 countries surveyed, the percentage of the South Korean public having a favorable image of the United States exceeded the percentage in only four other countries.) Whatever one thinks about the US military presence on the peninsula, a process of local tension de-escalation not accompanied by the elimination of the broader threat to global stability posed by the North Korean nuclear weapons and missiles programs is at a minimum a recipe for bilateral political tension between Seoul and Washington.

These are big issues and beyond the scope of this policy analysis. They will be set aside for the remainder of the chapter to concentrate on the economic policy issues. In the memorable words of that fictional San Francisco detective, "Dirty" Harry Callaghan, "A man has got to know his limitations."

The Economics of Engagement

In the five years since the 1997 crisis, South Korea has made better progress than any other country in Asia (Japan included) in addressing its economic problems (Noland 2002b). As Arthur Alexander (2003) has demonstrated, corporate leverage has fallen to less than half its precrisis level, the rate of return on capital has increased, and the share of corporate "winners" (low leverage, above average profits) has more than doubled.

In the financial sector, the share of bad loans has been driven below 3 percent to its lowest level ever from a high of more than 15 percent in March 2000, and the capital adequacy of South Korean banks exceeds 10 percent on the Bank of International Settlements (BIS) standard. The result of this successful restructuring has been continued improvements in the country's credit rating. In the past five years the country has attracted more foreign investment than in the previous 50 combined.

The world is in the midst of a technological revolution that is significantly improving productivity, organizational relationships within and among firms, and the distribution of income and wealth, and South Korea has adopted information technology faster than any other economy in Asia and leads the world in broadband access.[1] Information technology is changing the structure of the South Korean economy. Given the rigidities and uncertain futures of the *chaebol*, since the 1997–98 crisis, there has been an upsurge in start-up activity and initial public offerings in the stock market, and the government is supporting the establishment of venture capital firms to support this process.[2] Admittedly, not all these new firms were in high technology, and the creative destruction of 1997–98 may have generated a temporary surge in new incorporations, nevertheless these developments demonstrate that business does not start and end with the *chaebol*. Indeed, these new firms are changing South Korean corporate culture as well, replacing the hierarchy and secrecy that have characterized the *chaebol* with greater flexibility and openness, partly due to generational change, as the ranks of South Korean corporate management are swelled by Western-educated business school graduates.

At the same time that South Korea is emerging as a global high-tech leader, it is also becoming an increasingly important supplier of cultural products to the rest of Asia. Today, South Korean pop culture (film, music, and fashion) trends are followed throughout Asia as keenly as (if not more than) Japanese styles. South Korean firms are aware of this and are attempting to build franchise value on the back of the country's cultural cachet, both at home and abroad. Interestingly, in Arthur Alexander's analysis of returns to capital in South Korea, the entertainment industry was the only sector classified as a "winner" (i.e., high profit, low leverage) in each year of his sample.

And while Seoul is not quite yet the Swinging London of the 1960s, profound political, economic, and social changes are clearly under way,

---

1. For a comprehensive analysis of the "New Economy," see the *Economic Report of the President*, Washington: Council of Economic Advisers, January 2001. Although this report is oriented toward the US economy, its insights have a broad applicability to South Korea. See Yusuf and Evenett (2002) for an Asia-centric discussion of the same issues and Noland (2002b) for South Korean illustrations.

2. See Seong (2003) on the venture capital business.

and the government's attempts to turn the country into an international business hub, however quixotic they may be, will reinforce this process.

Yet, regardless of its economic progress or policy stance, South Korea remains vulnerable to the vagaries of North Korean behavior. In June 2003, Standard and Poor's (S&P), which is in the business of assessing risk on a cross-nationally comparable basis, issued a report reading in part "No rated sovereign . . . faces a more serious military threat than the menace that North Korea poses to South Korea. Among investment-grade sovereigns, the State of Israel and Taiwan face serious geopolitical risks, but the danger is less present. In the case of South Korea, the risk comes from a failed state with nuclear weapons that must extort money with military threats to prop up its regime" (Standard and Poor's 2003, 3). S&P went on to explain that this situation exerts a dampening effect on South Korean bond ratings.

Moreover, it is precisely South Korea's greater integration with the rest of the world that creates new vulnerabilities in this context. Financially, South Korea is more integrated into the world economy now than it was at the time of the 1994 nuclear crisis. Foreigners are major players in the capital markets, accounting for nearly 40 percent of stock market transactions, and South Korean residents have greater opportunities to move their funds abroad. The use by South Korean financial firms of off–balance sheet transactions and financial derivatives, which did not exist in 1994, is expanding rapidly. While it is true that the South Korean stock market actually rose during that earlier crisis, the expanded role of foreign participants and the increased complexity of the financial transactions mean that the market today is far less susceptible to political intervention than it was a decade ago.

The popular image of capital flight occurring when foreigners flee for the exits is belied by historical experience the world over—almost invariably it is the better-informed locals who are out the door first. The Bank of Korea (BOK) data reveal that during periods of uncertainty, while foreigners were net buyers in the stock market, South Koreans were net sellers. And although at present there is no indication of capital flight— enabling mechanisms that did not exist in 1994 are in place today— the South Korean population is badly split with respect to its attitudes toward the North, and older South Koreans, who evince the greatest wariness toward North Korea, are the predominant owners of the country's savings.

South Korea should do two things. First, commit to the principle that engagement should be done on efficient, transparent terms. The fundamental issue is that as long as the state maintains direct and indirect influence over specific capital allocation decisions by financial intermediaries, it will be tempted to use this influence to promote its policy toward the North. The Hyundai Asan corruption trials in which five South Korean government officials were convicted of illegally channeling funds through the Korea Development Bank to Hyundai Asan for use in the North is exhibit A in this regard.[3] Subsidization of engagement with the North can be justified from a social standpoint (it may promote evolutionary economic and political change in the North), but it should be done as neutrally as possible with respect to specific projects and firms. The simplest way of accomplishing this would be to put provisions into the tax code that would create an incentive for South Korean firms to invest in the North instead of moving operations offshore to other destinations such as China and Southeast Asia. In contrast to implicit hidden subsidies and political quid pro quos delivered through the public-sector financial institutions, this approach would be a way to capture the possible social benefits of engagement with the North on the basis of microeconomic efficient behavior of private firms. Market-compatible engagement would have the added benefit of encouraging learning on the part of the North Koreans for whom much of their interaction with the outside world has been on nonmarket terms, either through aid agencies, politically subsidized activities by South Korean firms, and fronts for intelligence-gathering activities. The notion that the road to riches is through the efficient transparent provision of services is a lesson that North Korean officials should be encouraged to learn.

Such a tax-based approach would also have the virtue of transparency. While one can argue that given the history of enmity and distrust between North and South Korea, public subsidization of Hyundai Asan's activities in the North was justifiable on the grounds that South Korea had to in effect offer a loss leader to get the process of engagement going, the illegal and nontransparent way in which the engagement policy of the Kim Dae-jung government was implemented has created a political backlash against engagement and arguably has made it more difficult to implement the policy in the long run.[4]

Second, while engaging, South Korea should prepare for the possibility of collapse. The North can be thought of as the world's largest contingent liability. The relevant policies could be thought of as those that are contingent on specific circumstances and those that are relatively invariant to the timing and specifics of an eventual North Korean collapse.

---

3. Cross-debt guarantees to Hyundai Asan, the subsidiary responsible for activities in North Korea, were an issue in the disintegration of the parent Hyundai group. The Kim Dae-jung government's commitment to engagement with the North was so great that Hyundai's activities, undertaken at a time when the conglomerate was under great financial strain, were begun with the intent to create a moral hazard for the South Korean government, which would be unable to resist bailing out the *chaebol* should it encounter economic difficulties. The issue of "too big to fail" is discussed further later.

4. A similar, though smaller-scale, scandal over alleged under-the-table payments to North Korea involving the Roh Moo-hyun government erupted in October 2003. See Barbara Demick, "Sunshine from North Korea Has Its Source in Cold, Hard Cash," *Los Angeles Times*, November 17, 2003.

The specific to-do list in a collapse scenario was discussed in the previous chapter. Here the focus is on building the preparatory foundation—the policies that would be desirable whether or not North Korea existed. The specter of North Korea simply underscores the desirability of their adoption.

For the South Korean economy to continue to prosper, it must improve its mechanisms of resource mobilization, allocation, and management. The overarching goal should be to improve the functioning of markets. For this to occur, accurate information must be accessible, property rights must be enforced, and agents should be motivated by efficiency, not political considerations. So what can the government do to improve the business climate and create a stronger, more flexible economy in light of possible future contingencies?

First, markets operate on information, and better information facilitates greater efficiency in the allocation of capital. There is a general need to improve the quality of financial transparency in the South Korean economy. This requires improved accounting rules and conventions, truly independent accounting firms capable of auditing accounts, and a regulator capable of enforcing the rules with respect to corporate accounting and financial-sector firms—South Korea has made considerable progress since the 1997–98 crisis in this regard. Independent bodies have been established to rewrite South Korean accounting rules, bringing them closer to the International Accounting Standards (IAS), though additional progress would be welcome.[5] The South Koreans explicitly rejected the Generally Accepted Accounting Principles (GAAP) widely used in the United States and expressed some pride that Americans were looking into South Korea's reform experience in the wake of their own accounting scandals.[6] The production of consolidated financial statements under improved accounting rules beginning in May 2002 is another positive move. Unfortunately these positive developments have been overshadowed by a massive accounting and political influence peddling scandal involving the SK Group, South Korea's third largest *chaebol*. Additional accounting legislation has been proposed in the National Assembly but has yet to be enacted.

These improvements in practices have been backed up with heightened penalties for violators and more stringent enforcement. To cite a few examples, in September 2000, the Financial Supervisory Commission threw the book at Santong, one of Daewoo's main accounting firms, for conniving with its clients to falsify audits. In February 2001, facing

---

5. To cite an example: If a bank sells a nonperforming loan with a provision that if the loan does not meet certain performance rules, the selling bank will buy back the loan from the purchaser; under South Korean accounting rules, the bank is allowed to completely remove the loan from its books, despite the contingent liability associated with the buy-back provision.

6. Kim Yon-se, "US Imitates Korea's Accounting Reforms," *Korea Times*, May 12, 2003.

expiring statutes of limitation, Seoul prosecutors charged 34 Daewoo executives and accountants, including former chairman Kim Woo-choong, with fraud, though there are questions as to how serious the government is about tracking down the fugitive industrialist.[7] In March 2002, financial regulators accused seven of the largest accounting firms with malpractice involving 13 corporate clients. The Securities and Futures Commission sought criminal charges against two of the accounting firms and recommended the suspension of 26 auditors.[8] In July 2002, the Financial Supervisory Service (FSS) sent external auditors to examine the books at 100 companies suspected of irregularities, resulting in a number of indictments and convictions for financial crimes (Graham 2003). Unfortunately, although the number of professionals is increasing, the lack of trained accountants and auditors remains a constraint on the system.

With improvements in transparency, it becomes possible to impose capital-market discipline on corporate management.[9] Two institutional developments would facilitate this. The establishment of outside boards of directors would create an "inside" check on management abuse. This alone is no panacea, however: South Korea has successfully put new laws on the books regarding corporate boards, but the problem has been in implementation in a number of cases—incumbent managements have stuffed the boards with pliant cronies or even government officials.

A second desirable innovation would be the creation of independent institutional investors capable of monitoring management and fostering a market for corporate control. Related to this are the rights and treatment of "minority shareholders." As Graham (2003) points out, this appellation is a bit of a misnomer, because in some cases the "minority shareholders" actually hold bigger financial stakes in these firms than the insiders (often the company founder and associated family members). A number of shareholders rights groups, including the People's Solidarity for Participatory Democracy (PSPD) and its Center for Economic Reform and the Center for Good Corporate Governance, have had limited success in suing corporations for a variety of malpractices, but the law on class action suits has hampered this effort (Noland 2000, chapter 6). Again, legislation to facilitate

---

7. Thus far, the government has not referred Kim's case to Interpol and instead has merely asked South Korean embassies in countries where the fugitive industrialist is thought to be hiding. Many believe that he would implicate large parts of the South Korean political elite in the web of corruption.

8. Five of the accused firms have partnerships with the Big Five global accountancy groups, including Arthur Andersen of Enron fame. The accused clients included subsidiaries of the LG and SK groups (Andrew Ward, "South Korean Audits Under Fire," *Financial Times*, March 16, 2002). The Korea Deposit Insurance Corporation followed up by suing five of the firms for compensation for public losses resulting from "improper accounting" at the Daewoo and Kohap groups and separately sued the chairman of Kohap (Graham 2003).

9. See Cho (2003) for an overview of South Korean corporate governance issues.

class action suits by minority shareholders and to protect shareholders from false disclosure, unfaithful accounting, and stock price manipulation awaits approval in the National Assembly.

The creation of truly independent institutional investors would reinforce such activity. To the extent that such institutional investors exist in South Korea, they tend to be affiliated with the major *chaebol*. It would be desirable to separate financial and industrial groups, but this is unlikely to happen, and in fact, the October 2001 easing of restrictions on *chaebol* ownership of financial institutions goes in precisely the opposite direction.

Foreign investors now account for nearly 40 percent of trading on the South Korean stock exchange, and there have been instances of cooperation between some foreign institutional investors and the nascent shareholder rights movement exerting some beneficial effect. But the alliance with foreign investors allowed the *chaebol* to tar the good governance groups with the nationalist brush, and despite the increasing role of foreign firms in the domestic funds management business, it still appears necessary and desirable to develop independent South Korean institutional investors.[10] Regrettably, prospects on this front are inauspicious.

Another potential source of discipline on corporate behavior is the banks, and their operation and financial health have been considerably improved, despite their current problems with excessive issuance of credit cards. As mentioned previously, tremendous progress has been made with respect to nonperforming loans (NPLs), even taking into account the growing importance of household lending and increasing rates of personal bankruptcy. The recovery rate on NPLs of more than 30 percent, though lower than what was achieved by the United States in its relatively smaller savings and loan crisis, is in the same league of successful banking system rehabilitations in Finland and Chile and far higher than the comparable figure for Japan over same period (IMF 2003, box 3). This improvement in financial health has been facilitated by industry restructuring and consolidation, which despite labor-union opposition greatly reduced previously existing overstaffing.

Beyond the balance sheet issue, there is the critical requirement that financial intermediaries change their behavior and make investment decisions on economic, not political, grounds. There are multiple grounds for optimism on this score. The government, which at the height of the crisis owned three-quarters of the banking system, has largely sold its holdings and effectively denationalized the industry. The practice of pressuring private banks to participate in bond underwriting schemes and bond stabilization funds organized by the Korea Development Bank, at the center of the controversy regarding subsidies to Hynix Semiconductor, has been ended by terminating these programs.

---

10. See Graham (1999) for an interesting proposal to use pension fund money to create independent institutional investors.

The entry of foreign investors and firms has brought with it new management approaches and technologies. Foreign participation in the financial system has been increased both through direct investment in South Korean banks and through management contracts with South Korean–owned banks.

And some of the measures introduced in the wake of the crisis appear to be at least modestly reducing the extent of cross-company financial links among *chaebol* firms, thus permitting investors to better separate good from bad *chaebol* businesses. Improvements in management have been reinforced by improvements in prudential regulation such as the introduction of "forward-looking criteria" in asset classification standards. The replacement of blanket deposit insurance, introduced during the crisis, in favor of a limited deposit insurance scheme should encourage the reallocation of saving toward better-managed intermediaries within the financial system itself. Commercial bank capital adequacy as measured by the BIS is over 10 percent. Less progress has been made with respect to nonbank financial intermediaries. It would be desirable for the FSS to continue its policy of scrutinizing the use of financial derivatives and off–balance sheet transactions by South Korean financial entities.

Even improved decision making will still generate failures, however, and the continued existence of capital-eating "zombie" firms, which exhibit persistent financial weakness, attests to the absence of functioning exit mechanisms. As detailed by Alexander (2003), one of the notable developments in the South Korean economy over the past several years has been increased differentiation of corporate performance. One aspect is the increasing prominence of "winners"—high-profit, low-leverage firms. Yet at the same time there is clearly a class of chronically weak firms, unable to generate sufficient earnings to cover the interest on their debt, accounting for perhaps 10 to 25 percent of the corporate sector (Alexander 2003, IMF 2003). These zombies must either be restructured to achieve profitability, or, if this is not possible, they must be closed—otherwise their continued existence sucks the lifeblood away from the truly efficient firms by competing with them for scarce capital and labor on the input side and depressing prices on the output side. The problem in South Korea, as one wag puts it, is that "the bankruptcy procedures are themselves bankrupt" (Graham 2003, 168).

When the crisis hit in 1997, South Korea, which after all had been growing robustly for 35 years, did not have a well-developed system for corporate failures. There simply had not been many failures, and many of those that had occurred had historically been handled through informal extrajudicial bank-led workouts, not formal bankruptcies. Lacking both the laws and the specialized courts to handle the wave of corporate failures in 1998, the government, as the owner of three-quarters of the crumbling banking system, faced the prospect of a politicized process of negotiations with delinquent borrowers, a situation former Prime Minister

Nam Duck-woo memorably described as "akin to having some [hospital] patients assume responsibility for the treatment of other patients" (Nam 2000, 37). In response, the government effectively normalized the informal procedures through the introduction of the corporate restructuring vehicle (CRV) and prepackaged bankruptcy (PB) to at least handle the relatively less politicized cases not involving the major *chaebol* or their subsidiaries (Graham 2003, Park 2003).

In the meantime, the government took direct responsibility for workouts of the major distressed borrowers. Unfortunately, the government was hesitant, reflecting the belief that some firms were "too big to fail," and a preference for trying to organize intra–South Korean solutions over selling assets to foreigners. One prominent example was the case of Daewoo Motors.[11] In 1998, as the Daewoo conglomerate was failing, it announced that it would sell much of its stake in Daewoo Motors to GM, with which it had historical ties, but GM exhibited a lack of interest and the sale was never consummated. After the Daewoo bankruptcy, GM offered to buy Daewoo Motors, but the South Korean government refused the offer and engaged in a fruitless negotiation with Ford. In the meantime, Daewoo Motors was kept by its creditors, most notably banks under direct or indirect state control. New loans extended to Daewoo Motors in the fall of 2000 temporarily preserved 50,000 jobs, at a cost of $80,000 per job. Even with this infusion of cash, internal documents indicated that Daewoo Motors would have to shed more than one-third of its workforce (Noland 2002b).

Delay has costs beyond the obvious one cited above. Firms are more than a collection of machinery. As time passed, the value of the automaker to any prospective buyer declined. Talented staff departed the firm. New product models were not developed. The retail distribution system atrophied. GM finally purchased Daewoo Motors in 2002 for around $400 million—roughly a tenth of what it had bid two years earlier.

Daewoo Motors is not the only example of this tendency. An ongoing case is Hynix Semiconductor, formerly Hyundai Electronics, which is at the center of US and EU allegations that the South Korean government has used its influence over the financial system to prop up Hynix to the detriment of US-based Micron Technology and Germany's Infineon.[12] (The implicit subsidization of Hynix also harms Samsung Electronics, probably South Korea's premier firm, but that is an internal matter.) For a time it appeared that the dispute would be resolved by Micron's offer to take over Hynix, which was supported by Hynix's creditors but scuttled

---

11. See Noland (2000, 2002b) and Graham (2003) for analyses of the "too big to fail" phenomenon in general and the Daewoo Motors case in particular. D.G. Lee (2003) also contains an analysis of Daewoo restructuring.

12. In the case of Hynix, the state-run Korea Development Bank agreed to purchase hundreds of millions of dollars of otherwise unsellable bonds. For a highly informative analysis of the Hynix situation, see Manyin, Cooney, and Grimmett (2003).

by the Hynix board. In November 2002, Micron filed a countervailing duty case against Hynix alleging that the South Korean government's actions amounted to an illegal subsidy, and on April 1, 2003, the Department of Commerce announced a preliminary countervailing duty of 57 percent against Hynix's chips. In the meantime, the European Union and Taiwan are pursuing similar complaints under their respective laws, and in April 2003, the European Union imposed a 33 percent countervailing duty on Hynix chips. It follows predictably that chip prices will rise in the United States and the European Union, helping Micron and Infineon, but hurting downstream users such as in those locations. Hynix will be forced to dump its chips in Asia, primarily hurting emerging Chinese producers but lowering costs to chip users in Asia, such as electronics assemblers in China and Southeast Asia. The firm's fortunes have been boosted by the worldwide rise in semiconductor prices, which has accompanied the global revival of the electronics sector, but in the long run, it will probably lose market share as its capital-starved plants lose competitiveness.

South Korea still has not developed the procedures (and perhaps the political will) to allow corporate failures to be resolved through a transparent legal process. The mechanisms introduced in the wake of the crisis were really stop-gap measures. However, the government has moved both to expand and improve the functioning of bankruptcy courts and to improve the law, for example, by unifying the existing three-track mechanism for resolving bankruptcies (Lim 2003). A draft Bankruptcy Act was circulated for public comment in November 2002, but the legislation that would streamline and strengthen the existing bankruptcy procedures languishes in the National Assembly.

The other aspect of an efficient exit mechanism is the existence of a functioning social safety net—otherwise understandable concern about job losses will inhibit the closure of unprofitable facilities. Again, in this regard South Korea has made considerable progress since the crisis, when its social safety net was really oriented toward the proverbial widows and orphans and had only a very narrowly targeted unemployment insurance scheme. Since then the government has made considerable strides, yet more remains to be done. As pointed out by Graham (2003) and the OECD (2003), the unemployment insurance system is limited to full-time workers who make up a declining percentage of the labor force as part-time and temporary work becomes increasingly common, which in turn is a reaction to existing labor laws that make full-time workers a quasi-fixed factor of production. One consequence is that the existing unemployment insurance system covers a shrinking share of the labor force. The 2003 OECD *Economic Survey of South Korea* contains a discussion of this issue along with other recommendations for labor-market reform.

The situation with regard to foreign investment is illustrative of these themes.[13] South Korea experienced a substantial increase in foreign direct investment (FDI) after the financial crisis, but this appears to have been in large part the result of minority-stake foreign investors buying out their cash-strapped South Korean partners—not new, greenfield investors or new mergers and acquisitions. (South Korea's historical inhospitality to foreign investment encouraged the development of minority-stake joint ventures as the primary form of investment—given the opacity of South Korean accounting at the time, these incumbent inside investors were the only foreigners who knew the true value of the assets that they were buying.) Once this one-time process of minority stakeholders buying out their South Korean partners was completed, the flow of foreign investment began to dry up, and it has fallen steadily since 2000.[14] As of that year, South Korea ranked 23rd out of 25 OECD member countries in stock of inward FDI as a share of GDP, besting only Japan and Iceland. And although some will rightly point out that there has been a slackening in cross-border investment worldwide, the decline in South Korea appears to be particularly pronounced. Why do foreign investors appear to be relatively uninterested in South Korea, despite the government's goal of turning the country into a regional economic hub?

They typically identify three barriers to investment in South Korea (two of which apply equally to domestic investors as well). Labor-market problems are the most widely cited impediments to investment in both surveys of US and Japanese investors and formal grievances filed with the South Korean government. This is ironic inasmuch as labor unrest is at least partly a product of the government's interventions in labor disputes and its financial-sector policies that ironically encourage labor militancy. The unwillingness of creditors (often ultimately the government) to impose hard budget constraints on management obviates any incentive for union leaders to compromise in negotiations—as long as the government is willing to bail out management, any union leader who compromised would be, in American parlance, a chump.

The stated goal of the incoming Roh Moo-hyun government to revitalize President Kim Dae-jung's Tripartite (business, labor, government) Commission has further raised concerns that South Korea may be headed toward a corporatist labor-market model along continental European lines. Policies and institutions matter: Although South Korea, the United States, and France all have similar unionization rates (South Korea's is actually the lowest at 11 percent), labor-market practices differ significantly be-

---

13. To be clear, the issue of foreign investment is used here for heuristic purposes—I do not believe that lack of foreign investment is the most important issue facing South Korea, just that it nicely illustrates some underlying issues.

14. The data on foreign investment in South Korea, while not in North Korea's league of unreliability, are problematic. See Noland (2003b) and Yun (2003) for more extensive discussions.

tween the United States and France.[15] Foreign investors have expressed concerns regarding issues such as restrictions on redundancies, mandatory severance pay, and the potential criminal liability of expatriate managers for a broad range of infractions.

The second impediment to investment is a lack of transparency in financial accounting. Its impact on FDI is particularly acute. In the 2002 A.T. Kearney annual survey of corporate executives, South Korea placed 21st in the FDI confidence index, lagging such countries as India, Poland, and Thailand. The consulting firm PricewaterhouseCoopers actually calculates an opacity index. South Korea ranked 31st out of 34, beating Russia, Turkey, and Indonesia but trailing countries such as Egypt and Romania. According to PwC's econometric model, if South Korea could achieve the average transparency level of the United States, Chile, the United Kingdom, and Singapore (the least opaque economies in North America, South America, Europe, and Asia, respectively)—admittedly a tall order—it would triple its FDI inflow. This is more than just theory or an econometric exercise. For example, at least one large institutional investor places South Korea in its "tier three/semi-transparent" category and imputes a significant "transparency risk premium" in its calculations of hurdle rates for investment in the South Korean economy.

The third barrier to foreign investment consists of financial, tax, and other regulatory problems that, for example, impede the repatriation of revenues by multinational firms to their home offices. Other impediments to foreign investment include "borrowed technology" (South Korean firms license technology extensively, and these licenses typically contain provisions that the license lapses if ownership of the licensee firm changes), and locational restrictions that primarily relate to measures undertaken to discourage geographical concentration in the area around Seoul.

It is important to recognize that these reforms are self-reinforcing: Reforms in the financial sector will encourage better results with respect to corporate decision making and labor-market outcomes, for example. Corporate bailouts through concessional loans by public-sector financial institutions discourage compromise on the part of unions. Situations in which managements do not face hard budget constraints encourage labor militancy. Likewise it is important that the Tripartite Commission not become the locus of efficiency-reducing corporatism as similar bodies have become in continental Europe.

Final Thoughts

The existence of North Korea and uncertainty about its future raise fundamental issues for South Korea. In many respects, South Korea will

---

15. See C.S. Lee (2003) for a survey of empirical work on labor practices and FDI inflows.

remain vulnerable to Kim Jong-il's whims, whatever it does. Yet regardless of what path North Korea follows, whether it experiences evolutionary or discontinuous political change, economic integration between North and South Korea is in the cards—the only deep uncertainty is whether it occurs abruptly or gradually.

Throughout the world, political leaders are asked to undertake actions that, at least in the short run, will increase economic distress in their societies. While the experts assure them that in the long run the policy castor oil will contribute to their economies' rejuvenation, political leaders are asked to make big decisions on the basis of essentially theoretical (if not theological) arguments about the behavior of markets. No politician could be expected to take on the painful task of economic restructuring with much enthusiasm, and it is not surprising that market participants are always on the lookout for backsliding. Perhaps the July 2002 economic policy changes in North Korea are the start of such a process there. These reforms differ fundamentally from the highly touted diplomatic openings of the last several years. Unlike the diplomatic initiatives, which really only affected a small number of elites, the economic policy changes affect everyone in the society. Make no mistake about it: North Korea has crossed the Rubicon from the realm of the elite to the realm of mass politics. Whether Kim Jong-il or his successors will be successful in either rejuvenating the economy or maintaining their political control in the face of profound changes at the grassroots level is an open question.

South Korean leaders face a set of choices that paradoxically at once put both more and less at risk than the decisions confronting their counterparts in the North. The South possesses both a stronger economy and a stronger polity (though sometimes reading the newspaper might lead one to believe otherwise). The decisions that the South's leadership must make are not the life and death decisions about personal and regime survival confronting the North. They are nevertheless profoundly critical decisions about how to preserve the elusive personal and national virtues of liberty, democracy, and self-determination while pursuing national reconciliation. As the late Muddy Waters sang, "You can't lose what you never had."

Yet the immediacy of the issues confronting South Korea's leaders in an odd way conveys its own advantages. Unlike their counterparts elsewhere, for South Koreans, envisioning the returns to careful preparation and reform need not be an act of faith or an exercise in imagination— they need only look across the demilitarized zone to see their once and future partners.

Data Appendix

In most cases, data on GDP per capita, growth, aid per capita, inflation, population, urbanization, growth rate of the urban population, population density, the share of fuel, ore, and metal exports in GDP, and unemployment are taken and calculated from the World Bank's *World Development Indicators 2003*. Aid per capita for the high-income countries in the samples is assumed to be zero. Aid figures for Taiwan are taken from the *Taiwan Statistical Data Book 2003* (Council of Economic Planning and Development 2003) measured as the total arrival amount of US aid for 1960–68 and are assumed to be zero thereafter. Data on openness and government share of real GDP are taken from *Penn World Tables version 6.1*. Data on latitude, legal origin, region, area, transition economies, landlocked countries, major export category, and ethno-linguistic fractionalization are taken from the Global Development Network Growth Database of the World Bank (Easterly and Sewadeh 2002) and in some cases supplemented with the *2003 CIA World Fact Book* and, for Taiwan, the *Taiwan Statistical Data Book 2003*. Data on religious fractionalization and combined ethno-linguistic and religious fractionalization are taken from Arnett (2001).

Per capita income data for North Korea are calculated by dividing the Bank of Korea's dollar estimate of GDP by its estimate of population.[1] Income data for Cuba and Romania are taken from *Penn World Tables version 6.1*.

---

1. See Bank of Korea Web site at www.bok.or.kr/bokis_attach/00000013/200308061752261.xls.

Several variables from Burnside and Dollar (1997), updated by Easterly, Levine, and Roodman (2003), were tried at various stages of the analysis. These include development aid, number of assassinations, institutional quality, budget surplus as a share of GDP, inflation, the Sachs-Warner openness index, and arms imports as a share of total imports lagged by one period. The data are reported in eight periods consisting of three-year intervals beginning in 1966 and ending in 1997. For 1960–69, the first period values were entered. For years within the intervals, the values for the period were entered (e.g., for 1970 to 1973, the second period values were entered). For 1994–2000, the eighth period values were entered. Of the variables tried, assassinations, inflation, and arms imports were significant under certain specifications. The data on assassinations and arms imports have significant limitations and the data on inflation from the *World Development Indicators* have substantially better coverage for our samples.

Coverage of Regressions

Regressions 3.1 and 3.2 cover 175 regime changes in 71 countries. Due to missing data and the censoring described below, the mean time at risk for countries in these regressions is approximately 35.6 years. Regressions 3.3 and 3.4 cover 149 regime changes in 70 countries. Data limitations and censoring reduced the mean time at risk for these countries to 32.7 years. Regression 3.5 covers 78 regime changes in 68 countries with a mean time at risk of 25.4 years. Regression 3.6 covers 68 regime changes in 22 countries with a mean time at risk of 34.6 years.

Risk Onset and Censoring

Several countries included in the samples were not independent by 1960, the beginning of the Polity IV regression samples. These countries are only considered at risk of experiencing regime change after independence. In addition, periods of state failure (defined in the text) are treated as censored.

Calculation of Trade Protection Measure

Data on trade taxes as a share of government revenue are taken from the International Monetary Fund's *Government Finance Statistics Yearbook 1991* and are calculated as follows: the total international taxes (line 6 in table A of the individual country tables in the yearbook) was divided by total government revenue plus grants (line I). This share is entered as a percentage in the dataset. While most data on trade taxes and government revenue are taken from 1981, data availability varies. Where 1981

Table A.1   Estimates for North Korea, 1990–2002

Year	Government share (percent)	Openness[a] (percent)	Urbanization (percent)	Trade taxes as a share of revenue (percent)	Aid per capita (percent)	Inflation (percent)
1990	33	20	74	17	11	2
1991	34	12	74	17	21	2
1992	40	13	74	17	19	2
1993	41	13	74	17	14	2
1994	33	12	74	17	11	2
1995	28	13	74	17	38	2
1996	26	18	74	17	24	2
1997	24	16	74	17	37	2
1998	22	11	74	17	33	2
1999	23	12	74	17	48	2
2000	23	16	74	17	73	2
2001	22	17	74	17	49	2
2002	22	17	74	17	56	2

a. Exports plus imports as a share of GDP.

Source: Author's calculations.

data are not available, they are taken from the closest available year, in some cases before but usually after 1981.

Legal Origins

Data on legal origins are taken from the Global Development Network Growth Database of the World Bank (Easterly and Sewadeh 2002). In general, the data are entered as fixed effects so that a given country has the same legal origin over the entire time of observation. There are two notable exceptions. First, the original data report Hungary as having a socialist legal origin. We allow Hungary to revert to a German legal system post-1989. Laos is also reported as socialist in the original data. We treat Laos as French pre-1976.

Hazard and Cumulative Hazard Calculations

The cumulative hazards reported in figure 2.2 are calculated by summing the hazard of regime change at time t for $1 \leq t \leq 41$ as estimated by substituting the mean values of the covariates into the model. The hazards of regime change in North Korea reported in figure 2.3 are calculated by substituting into the model data on GDP, growth, latitude, and legal origin along with estimates of government share, openness, urbanization, trade taxes as a share of revenue, aid per capita, and inflation (table A.1).

References

Acemoglu, Daron, James A. Robinson, and Simon Johnson. 2001. The Colonial Origins of Comparative Development. *American Economic Review* 91, no. 5: 1369–1401.

Ahn, Byung-joon. 1994a. The Man Who Would Be Kim. *Foreign Affairs* 73, no. 6: 94–108.

Ahn, Byung-joon. 1994b. Korea's Future after Kim Il-sung. *Korea and World Affairs* (Fall): 442–72.

Albright, Madeleine. 2003. *Madame Secretary.* New York: Miramax.

Alesina, Alberto, Sule Özler, Nouriel Roubini, and Philip Swagel. 1996. Political Instability and Economic Growth. *Journal of Economic Growth* 1: 193–215.

Alesina, Alberto, Arnaud Devleeschauwer, William Easterly, Sergio Kurlat, and Romain Wacziag. 2002. Fractionalization. *Harvard Institute of Economic Research Discussion Paper* 1959. Cambridge, MA: Harvard University.

Alexander, Arthur. 2003. Korea's Capital Investment. *Special Studies Series* 2. Washington: Korea Economic Institute of America.

Armstrong, Charles. 1998. A Socialism in Our Own Style: North Korean Ideology in a Post-Communist Era. In *North Korean Foreign Relations,* ed., Samuel S. Kim. Hong Kong: Oxford University Press.

Armstrong, Charles. 2002. *The North Korean Revolution.* Ithaca, NY: Cornell University Press.

Arnett, Anthony. 2001. Social Fractionalization, Political Instability, and the Size of Government. *IMF Staff Papers* 48, no. 3. Washington: International Monetary Fund.

Åslund, Anders, Peter Boone, and Simon Johnson. 1996. How To Stabilize: Lessons from Post-Communist Countries. *Brookings Papers on Economic Activity* 1996: 1: 217–313. Washington: Brookings Institution.

Bae, Jin-young. 1996. The Fiscal Burden of Korean Reunification and Its Impact on South Korea's Macroeconomic Stability. *Joint U.S.-Korea Academic Studies* 6: 185–202.

Barry, Mark Philip. 1996. Contemporary American Relations with North Korea: 1987–1994. Unpublished dissertation. Woodrow Wilson Department of Government and Foreign Affairs, University of Virginia, May.

Bennett, D. Scott. 1999. Parametric Models, Duration Dependence, and Time-Varying Data Revisited. *American Journal of Political Science* 43, no. 1: 256–70.

Berkowitz, Daniel, Katharina Pistor, and Jean-Francois Richard. 2000. Economic Development, Legality, and the Transplant Effect. *CID Working Paper* No. 39. Cambridge, MA: Center for International Development, Harvard University.

Box-Steffensmeier, Janet M., and Bradford S. Jones. 1997. Time is of the Essence: Event History Models in Political Science. *American Journal of Political Science* 41, no. 4: 1414–61.

Box-Steffensmeier, Janet M., and Christopher J.W. Zorn. 2001. Duration Models in Political Science. *American Journal of Political Science* 45, no. 4: 972–88.

Brinton, Crane. 1966. *Anatomy of a Revolution*. New York: Random House.

Bueno de Mesquita, Bruce, and Jongryn Mo. 1997. Prospects for Economic Reform and Political Stability. In *North Korea After Kim Il Sung*, ed., Thomas H. Hendriksen and Jongryn Mo. Stanford, CA: Hoover Institution.

Burnside, Craig, and David Dollar. 1997. Aid, Policies, and Growth. *Policy Research Working Paper* 1777. Washington: World Bank.

Burton, Charles. 2003. Solving the DPRK Conundrum. *CanKor* #139, Special Edition, 24 October.

Chirot, Daniel. 1996. The East European Revolutions of 1989. In *Revolutions* (2d ed.), ed., Jack A. Goldstone. Fort Worth: Harcourt Brace.

Cho, Myeong-Hyeong. 2003. Reform of Corporate Governance. In *Economic Crisis and Corporate Restructuring in Korea*, ed., Stephan Haggard, Wonhyuk Lim, and Euysung Kim. Cambridge, MA: Cambridge University Press.

Choi, Wan-kyu. 1998. The Current State and Tasks of the Study of Change in the North Korean Political System. In *Understanding Regime Dynamics in North Korea*, ed., Chung-in Moon. Seoul: Yonsei University Press.

Chung, Yun Ho. 2003. The Prospects of Economic Reform in North Korea and the Direction of Its Economic Development. *Vantage Point* 26, no. 5 (May): 43–53.

Cohn, Norman. 1970. *The Pursuit of the Millennium* (revised). New York: Oxford University Press.

Collier, Paul, and Anke Hoeffler. 2002. *Greed and Grievance in Civil War*. Centre for the Study of African Economies WPS/2002-01 (March). Oxford, UK: Centre for the Study of African Economies

Collins, Robert. 1996. Patterns of Collapse in North Korea. *The Combined Forces Command C5 Civil Affairs Newsletter*. Seoul, Korea (January).

Council of Economic Planning and Development, Republic of China. 2003. *Taiwan Statistical Data Book 2003*. www.cepd.gov.tw/english/file/databook2003.pdf (p. 249).

Cumings, Bruce. 1995. *Divided Korea: United Future*. New York: Foreign Policy Association.

Cumings, Bruce. 1997. *Korea's Place in the Sun*. New York: Norton.

Deutch, John. 1996. Testimony before the Senate Select Intelligence Committee Report on the CIA and National Security. Washington: United States Senate (December 11).

Djankov, Simeon, Rafael LaPorta, Florencio Lopez-de-Silvanes, and Andrei Shliefer. 2002. Courts: The Lex Mundi Project. *NBER Working Paper Series* 8890. Cambridge, MA: National Bureau of Economic Research.

Dollar, David, and Jakob Svensson. 2000. What Explains the Success or Failure of Structural Adjustment Programmes? *Economic Journal* 110 (October): 894–917.

Easterly, William, Ross Levine, and David Roodman. 2003. *New Data, New Doubts: Revisiting 'Aid, Policies, and Growth.'* Working Paper 26. Washington: Center for Global Development.

Easterly, William, and Ross Levine. 1997. Africa's Growth Tragedy: Policies and Ethnic Divisions. *Quarterly Journal of Economics* CXII, no. 4: 1203–50.

Easterly, William, and Mirvat Sewadeh. 2002. Global Development Network Growth Database. www.worldbank.org/research/growth/GDNdata.htm (accessed January 16).

Eberstadt, Nicholas. 1995. *Korea Approaches Reunification*. Armonk, NY: M.E. Sharpe.

Eberstadt, Nicholas. 1997. Hastening Korean Reunification. *Foreign Affairs* (March/April): 77–92.

Eberstadt, Nicholas. 1998. Is Contemporary North Korea a 'Pre-Revolutionary Polity?': A Summary of Findings. Photocopy (March).

Eberstadt, Nicholas. 1999. *The End of North Korea*. Washington: American Enterprise Institute.

Elbadawi, Ibrahim, and Nicholas Sambanis. 2002. How Much War Will We See? *Journal of Conflict Resolution* 46, no. 3: 307–33.

Forbes, Kristin J. 2000. A Reassessment of the Relationship Between Inequality and Growth. *American Economic Review* 90, no. 4: 869–87.

Foster-Carter, Aidan. 1992. Korea's Coming Unification. *Economist Intelligence Unit M212* (April). London: Economist Intelligence Unit.

Foster-Carter, Aidan. 1994. Korea: Sociopolitical Realities of Reuniting a Divided Nation. In *One Korea?* ed., Thomas H. Hendricksen and Kyong-soo Lho. Stanford: Hoover Institution Press.

Foster-Carter, Aidan. 1997a. How Long Can North Korea Go On Like This? *The Economics of Korean Reunification* 2, no. 1: 28–35.

Foster-Carter, Aidan. 1997b. North Korea in Retrospect. In *The Korean Peninsula in Transition*, ed., Dae Hwan Kim and Tat Yan Kong. London: Macmillan.

Foster-Carter, Aidan. 1997c. What Will Happen in North Korea? Flemings Research, Global Emerging Markets, Hong Kong.

Foster-Carter, Aidan. 1998a. North Korea: All Roads Lead to Collapse. In *Economic Integration of the Korean Peninsula*, ed., Marcus Noland. Washington: Institute for International Economics.

Foster-Carter, Aidan. 1998b. Regime Dynamics in North Korea. In *Understanding Regime Dynamics in North Korea*, ed., Chung-in Moon. Seoul: Yonsei University Press.

Frank, Ruediger. 2003. A Socialist Market Economy in North Korea? Systemic Restrictions and a Quantitative Analysis. Photocopy. Columbia University, New York.

Funke, Michael, and Holger Strulik. 2002. Growth and Convergence in a Two-Region Model: The Hypothetical Case of Korean Unification. *IMF Working Paper* No. 02/26. Washington: International Monetary Fund.

Goldstone, Jack A. 1986. Introduction. In *Revolutions*, ed., Jack A. Goldstone. San Diego: Harcourt Brace Jovanovich.

Graham, Edward M. 1999. A Radical but Workable Restructuring Plan for South Korea. *International Economic Policy Briefs* 99-2. Washington: Institute for International Economics.

Graham, Edward M. 2003. *Reforming Korea's Industrial Conglomerates*. Washington: Institute for International Economics.

Green, Michael. 1997. North Korea Regime Crisis. *The Korean Journal of Defense Analysis* 9, no. 2: 7–25.

Gurr, Ted. 1970. *Why Men Rebel*. Princeton: Princeton University Press.

Hankiss, Elemér. 1994. European Paradigms: East and West, 1945–1994. *Daedalus* 123, no. 3: 115–27.

Hegre, Håvard. 2003. *Disentangling Democracy and Development as Determinants of Armed Conflict*. Washington: World Bank.

Hirshleifer, Jack. 1963. Disaster and Recovery: A Historical Survey. *Memorandum RM-3079-PR*. Santa Monica, CA: The RAND Corporation (April).

Holmes, Stephen. 1996. Cultural Legacies or State Collapse? In *Post-communism*, ed., Michael Mandelbaum. New York: Council on Foreign Relations.

Hufbauer, Gary C., Jeffrey J. Schott, and Kimberly Ann Elliott. 1990. *Economic Sanctions Reconsidered* (2d ed.). Washington: Institute for International Economics.

Huh, Moon-young. 1996. The Stability and Durability of the Kim Jong-il Regime. *The Korean Journal of National Unification* 5: 65–81.

Hunter, Helen-Louise. 1999. *Kim Il-sung's North Korea*. Westport, CT: Praeger.

Huntington, Samuel P. 1968. *Political Order in Changing Societies*. New Haven, CT: Yale University Press.

IMF (International Monetary Fund). 2003. Republic of Korea: 2002 Article IV Consultation. *IMF Country Report* 03/79 (March). Washington: International Monetary Fund.

Kim, Kyung-won. 1996. No Way Out: North Korea's Impending Collapse. *Harvard International Review* XVIII, no. 2 (Spring): 22–71.

Kim, Pyung-joo. 1998. Monetary Integration and Stabilization in the Unified Korea. In *Policy Priorities for the Unified Korean Economy*, ed., Il Sakong and Kwang-suk Kim. Seoul: Institute for Global Economics.

Kim, Sung-chull. 1996. The Development of Systemic Dissonance in North Korea. *The Korean Journal of National Unification* 5: 83–109.

Knack, Stephen. 2000. Aid Dependence and the Quality of Governance. *World Bank Development Research Group Working Paper* 2396 (July). Washington: World Bank.

Koh, B.C. 1998. American Perspectives on Regime Dynamics in North Korea. In *Understanding Regime Dynamics in North Korea*, ed., Moon Chung-in. Seoul: Yonsei University Press.

Kuran, Timur. 1989. Sparks and Prairie Fires: A Theory of Unanticipated Political Revolutions. *Public Choice* 61, no. 1: 41–74.

Kuran, Timur. 1995a. The Inevitability of Future Revolutionary Surprises. *American Journal of Sociology* 100: 1528–51.

Kuran, Timur. 1995b. *Private Truths, Public Lies: The Social Consequence of Preference Falsification*. Cambridge, MA: Harvard University Press.

Laney, James T. 1995. Remarks to the Asian Society. Washington, 3 May.

Lankov, Andrei. 2003. Pyongyang: Rules of Engagement. *Pacific Review* 16, no. 4: 617–26.

LaPorta, Rafael, Florencio Lopez-de-Silanes, Andrei Shleifer, and Robert W. Vishny. 1999. The Quality of Government. *Journal of Law, Economics, and Organization* 15: 222–79.

Lau, Lawrence J., Yingi Qian, and Gérard Roland. 2000. Reform Without Losers: An Interpretation of China's Dual-Track Approach to Transition. *Journal of Political Economy* 108, no. 1: 120–43.

Leamer, Edward E. 1983. Let's Take the 'Con' out of Econometrics. *American Economic Review* 73, no. 1: 31–43.

Lee, Chang-soo. 2003. The Effect of Labor Market Institutions on FDI Inflows. *KIEP Working Paper* 03-09 (October). Seoul: Korea Institute for International Economic Policy.

Lee, Dong Gull. 2003. The Restructuring of Daewoo. In *Economic Crisis and Corporate Restructuring in Korea*, ed., Stephan Haggard, Wonhyuk Lim, and Euysung Kim. Cambridge, MA: Cambridge University Press.

Lee, Jung-chul. 2002. The Implications of North Korea's Reform Program and Its Effects on State Capacity. *Korea and World Affairs* 26, no. 3: 357–64.

Lee, Young-sun. 1995. Is Korean Unification Possible? Originally published in Korean in *Shin Dong—A Monthly*, May; English translation appeared in *Korea Focus* 3, no. 3 (May/June): 5–21.

Lho, Kyongsoo. 1999. The Democratic People's Republic of Korea in 2003: Soft Landing or Collapse? In *North Korean Scenarios (1999-2003) and Responses of the European Union*, ed., Christopher Dashwood and Kay Möller. Baden-Baden: Nomos Verlagsgesellschaft.

Lim, Youngjae. 2003. The Corporate Bankruptcy System and the Economic Crisis. In *Economic Crisis and Corporate Restructuring in Korea*, ed., Stephan Haggard, Wonhyuk Lim, and Euysung Kim. Cambridge, MA: Cambridge University Press.

Luttwak, Edward. 1979. *Coup d'Etat*. Cambridge, MA: Harvard University Press.

Maddison, Angus. 2003. *The World Economy: Historical Statistics*. OECD Development Centre Studies. Paris: OECD.

Mahoney, Paul G. 2001. The Common Law and Economic Growth: Hayek Might Be Right. *Journal of Legal Studies* 30, no. 2: 305–25.

Manyin, Mark E. 2000. North Korea-Japan Relations: The Normalization Talks and the Compensation/Reparations Issue. *CRS Report for Congress* (21 April). Washington: Congressional Research Service.

Manyin, Mark E., Stephen Cooney, and Jeanne J. Grimmett. 2003. The Semiconductor Industry and South Korea's Hynix Corporation. *CRS Report for Congress* (13 March). Washington: Congressional Research Service.

Maxwell, Major David A. 1996. Catastrophic Collapse in North Korea. United States Special Forces, School of Advanced Military Studies, United States Army Command and General Staff College Fort Leavenworth, Kansas—Second Term AY 95-96. www.kimsoft.com/korea/maxwell.htm.

Michell, Anthony. 1998. The Current North Korean Economy. In *Economic Integration on the Korean Peninsula*, ed., Marcus Noland. Washington: Institute for International Economics.

Munck, Gerardo L. 1996. Disaggregating Political Regime. *Kellogg Institute for International Studies Working Paper no. 228* (August). South Bend: University of Notre Dame.

Nam, Duck-woo. 2000. Time to Reassess Economic Restructuring. *Korea Focus* 8, no. 6 (November-December).

Nam, Sung-wook. 2003. Moves Toward Economic Reforms. *Vantage Point* 26, no. 10: 18–22.

Newcombe, William. 2003. Reflections on North Korea's Economic Reform. *Korea's Economy 2003*, volume 19. Washington: Korea Economic Institute of America.

Noland, Marcus. 1997. Why North Korea Will Muddle Through. *Foreign Affairs* 76, no. 4: 105–18.

Noland, Marcus. 1998. Introduction. In *Economic Integration on the Korean Peninsula*, ed., Marcus Noland. Washington: Institute for International Economics.

Noland, Marcus. 2000. *Avoiding the Apocalypse: The Future of the Two Koreas.* Washington: Institute for International Economics.

Noland, Marcus. 2001. Between Collapse and Revival: A Reinterpretation of the North Korean Economy. www.iie.com/publications/papers/noland0201-2.htm.

Noland, Marcus. 2002a. The Future of North Korea's Economic Reform. *Korean Journal of Defense Analysis* 14, no. 2: 73–90.

Noland, Marcus 2002b. Economic Reform in South Korea. www.iie.com/publications/papers/noland0402.htm

Noland, Marcus. 2003a. *Famine and Reform in North Korea.* Working Paper 03-5. Washington: Institute for International Economics.

Noland, Marcus. 2003b. Economic Ties in the Evolving U.S.-South Korea Relationship. In *The Strategic Importance of U.S.-South Korean Economic Relations NBR Special Report No. 4.* Seattle: National Bureau of Asian Research (October).

Noland, Marcus, Sherman Robinson, and Ligang Liu. 1998. The Costs and Benefits of Korean Unification. *Asian Survey* (August): 801–14.

Noland, Marcus, Sherman Robinson, and Ligang Liu. 1999. The Economics of Korean Unification. *Journal of Policy Reform* 3: 255–99.

Noland, Marcus, Sherman Robinson, and Tao Wang. 2000a. Rigorous Speculation: The Collapse and Revival of the North Korean Economy. *World Development* (October): 1767–87.

Noland, Marcus, Sherman Robinson, and Tao Wang. 2000b. Modeling Korean Unification. *Journal of Comparative Economics* (June): 400–21.

Oberdorfer, Don. 1997. *The Two Koreas.* Reading, MA: Addison-Wesley.

Organisation for Economic Cooperation and Development (OECD). 2003. *Korea.* Paris: OECD.

Oh, Kongdan, and Ralph C. Hassig. 2000. *North Korea Through the Looking Glass.* Washington: Brookings Institution.

Oh, Seung-yul. 2003. Changes in the North Korean Economy: New Policies and Limitations. *Korea's Economy 2003,* volume 19. Washington: Korea Economic Institute of America.

Pack, Howard, and Janet Rothenberg Pack. 1990. Is Foreign Aid Fungible: The Case of Indonesia. *Economic Journal* (March): 188–94.

Pack, Howard, and Janet Rothenberg Pack. 1993. Foreign Aid and the Question of Fungibility. *Review of Economics and Statistics* LXXV, no. 2: 258–65.

Park, Han S. 1998. Human Needs, Human Rights, and Regime Legitimacy. In *Understanding Regime Dynamics in North Korea*, ed., Moon Chung-in. Seoul: Yonsei University Press.

Park, Lt. Col. Jae-won. 1997. Possibility of North Korean Collapse. www.globalsecurity.org/military/library/report/1997/park.htm

Park, Kyung Suh. 2003. Bank-led Corporate Restructuring. In *Economic Crisis and Corporate Restructuring in Korea*, ed., Stephan Haggard, Wonhyuk Lim, and Euysung Kim. Cambridge, MA: Cambridge University Press.

Park, Suhk Sam, and Ralf Müller. 2001. Directions in the Financial Integration of South and North Korea. Seoul: Bank of Korea (October).

Perotti, Roberto. 1996. Growth, Income Distribution, and Democracy. *Journal of Economic Growth* 1: 149–87.

Perry, William J. 1999. Review of United States Policy toward North Korea: Findings and Recommendations. www.state.gov/regions/eap/991012_northkorea_rpt.html

Polity IV Project. 2000. Polity IV Dataset. College Park, MD: Center for International Development and Conflict Management, University of Maryland.

Pollack, Jonathan, and Chung-min Lee. 1999. *Preparing for Korean Unification*. Santa Monica, CA: RAND.

Przeworski, Adam, Michael E. Alvarez, José Antonio Cheibub, and Fernando Limongi. 2000. *Democracy and Development*. Cambridge, MA: Cambridge University Press.

RINU (Research Institute for National Unification). 1996. *Evaluating the Crisis Level and Prospective Regime Durability in the Communist Regime of the DPRK* [In Korean]. Seoul: Research Institute for National Unification (December).

Roy, Denny. 1998. North Korea As an Alienated State. *Survival* 38, no. 4: 22–36.

Sachs, Jeffrey. 1995. Reforms in Eastern Europe and the Former Soviet Union in Light of the East Asian Experience. *Journal of the Japanese and International Economies* 9 (December): 454–85.

Scalapino, Robert. 1992a. Trends in North-South Relations. *RINU Newsletter* 1, no. 1.

Scalapino, Robert. 1992b. *The Last Leninists: The Uncertain Future of Asia's Communist States*. Washington: Center for Strategic and International Studies.

Scalapino, Robert. 1995. Foreword. In *Korea Approaches Unification*, ed., Nicholas Eberstadt. Armonk, NY: M.E. Sharpe.

Scott, James C. 1976. *The Moral Economy of the Peasant*. New Haven, CT: Yale University Press.

Seong, Somi. 2003. Prospects of Korean Venture Business and Cooperation with Silicon Valley Firms. Paper presented at the symposium titled The United States and South Korea: Reinvigorating the Partnership, Stanford University, October 23–24.

Sinn, Gerlinde, and Hans-Werner Sinn. 1996. What Can Korea Learn from German Unification? In *Middle Powers in the Age of Globalization*, ed., Byong-Moo Hwang and Young Kwan Yoon. KAIS International Conference Series No. 5. Seoul: Korean Association of International Studies.

Skidelsky, Robert. 1996. The State and the Economy. In *Post-communism*, ed., Michael Mandelbaum. New York: Council on Foreign Relations

Skocpol, Theda. 1979. *States and Social Revolutions*. Cambridge, MA: Cambridge University Press.

Snyder, Scott. 1999. *Negotiating on the Edge*. Washington: US Institute for Peace.

Standard and Poor's. 2003. Korea (Republic of). New York: Standard and Poor's (June 9).

Suh, Jae Jean. 1997. Social Changes in North Korea and the Stability of the Kim Jong-il Regime. *Korea Focus* 5, no. 4: 51–62.

Suh, Jae Jean. 1998. Class Conflict and Regime Crisis in North Korea. In *Understanding Regime Dynamics in North Korea*, ed., Moon Chung-in. Seoul: Yonsei University Press.

Suh, Jae Jean, and Byoung-lo P. Kim. 1994. Prospects for Changes in the Kim Jong-il Regime. *Series No. 2 Policy Studies Report.* Seoul: Research Institute for National Unification.

Svensson, Jakob. 1999. Aid, Growth, and Democracy. *Economics and Politics* 11, no. 3 (November): 275–98.

Svensson, Jakob. 2000. Foreign Aid and Rent-Seeking. *Journal of International Economics* 51, no. 2: 437–61.

Tilly, Charles. 1978. *From Mobilization to Revolution.* Reading, MA: Addison-Wesley.

Trimberger, Ellen Kay. 1978. *Revolution from Above.* New Brunswick, NJ: Transaction Books.

Van den Berg, Gerard J. 2000. Duration Models: Specification, Identification, and Multiple Durations. In *Handbook of Econometrics* volume 5, ed., J.J. Heckman and E.E. Leamer. Amsterdam: North Holland.

Von Hippel, David, and Peter Hayes. 1998. DPRK Energy Sector: Current Status and Scenarios for 2000 and 2005. In *Economic Integration of the Korean Peninsula,* Special Report 10, ed., Marcus Noland. Washington: Institute for International Economics.

Watrin, Christian. 1998. Monetary Integration and Stabilization Policy: The German Case. In *Policy Priorities for the Unified Korean Economy,* ed., Il SaKong and Kwang Suk Kim. Seoul: Institute for Global Economics.

Williams, James H., Peter Hayes, and David Von Hippel. 1999. Fuel and Famine: North Korea's Rural Energy Crisis. Paper presented to the Pentagon Study Group on Japan and Northeast Asia, Washington, October 22.

Wolf, Holger. 1998. Korean Unification: Lessons from Germany. In *Economic Integration of the Korean Peninsula,* Special Report 10, ed., Marcus Noland. Washington: Institute for International Economics.

World Food Program. 2003a. Public Distribution System (PDS) in DPRK. DPR Korea Country Office, May 21.

World Food Program. 2003b. Wide Ranging Reforms Are Introduced. DPR Korea Country Office.

Young, Soogil, Chang-Jae Lee, and Hyoungsoo Zang. 1998. Preparing for the Economic Integration of Two Koreas: Policy Challenges to South Korea. In *Economic Integration of the Korean Peninsula,* Special Report 10, ed., Marcus Noland. Washington: Institute for International Economics.

Yun, Mikyung. 2003. Foreign Direct Investment and Corporate Restructuring after the Crisis. In *Economic Crisis and Corporate Restructuring in Korea,* ed., Stephan Haggard, Wonhyuk Lim, and Euysung Kim. Cambridge, MA: Cambridge University Press.

Yusuf, Shahid, and Simon J. Evenett. 2002. *How Can Asia Compete?* Washington: World Bank.

Index

accelerated failure time (AFT), 30
accounting rules, South Korean, 76, 76n
ADB. *See* Asian Development Bank
  (ADB)
administrative decentralization, 46
Afghanistan, 7
African National Congress (ANC), 11–12
Agreed Framework (October 1994), 15, 59
agricultural sector, 51
  employment in, 49
  prices in, 48–49
aid, 18
  from China, 62
  data on, 85–86
  effect on political stability, 61–63, 62n
  food, 61
  from Japan, 56n, 58n
  misappropriation of, 62
  from multilateral development banks, 59,
    59n, 69
  seeking of, 46
  from South Korea, 58–59, 62, 65, 75
  from United States, 58, 58n, 62
Albright, Madeleine, 2
alienated state, 11, 11n
"anarcholiberalism," 8
"apparatchik capitalism," 8, 62
apparel exports, 60n
Arthur S. Banks Cross National Time-Series
  Data Archive, 29
Asian Development Bank (ADB), 56, 58
automakers, 80
Azhari, Gholam Reza, 45

Bani-Sadr, Abolhassan, 45
banking system
  Chinese, 48
  South Korea, 78–79
Bank of International Settlements, 73
Bank of Korea (BOK), 21, 38, 74
  data from, 85, 85n
Bankruptcy Act, 81
bankruptcy procedures, 79–81
Barzagan, Mehdi, 4
Beijing (China), 18
Belarus, 8, 12, 62
BOK. *See* Bank of Korea (BOK)
bond markets, government, 67
bonds, 52, 52n
  unification, 67
border regions, political sanctuary in, 16
borrowed technology, 83
Botha, P.W., 11
Brezhnev, Leonid, 7
broadband access, 73
Bush, George W., 3, 18, 41, 58
business-government relations, in South
  Korea, 61

cabinet reshuffle, September 2003, 46
Cambodia, 59n
capital flight, 74
Castro, Fidel, 25
Catholic Church, 11, 16
Ceauşescu, Nikolai, 6, 25
censoring, 86

centrally planned economies (CPEs), 68–69
chaebol, 55, 69, 73, 78
Chile, 78, 83
China, 44
    aid from, 62
    banking system, 48
    economic integration between North Korea
        and, 56*n*, 57
    militarization in, 8
    military coordination with South Korea and
        the United States, 67–68, 72
    political sanctuary in, 16, 18
    reform process in, 12, 46–49, 46*n*, 54, 62
Christianity, 16
civil liberties, stifling of, in South Korea, 71
civil war, 64
Clinton administration, 15
collapse, 12–19
    versus continuation of Kim regime, 2, 13–14
    definition of, 2–3, 2*n*
    of East Germany, 7
    economic, definition of, 3*n*
    effect on South Korea, 65–67, 75–76
    nonrevolutionary, 12
    possibility of, and economic distress, 15–16,
        17*n*, 19
    predictions of, after death of Kim Il-sung,
        12, 12*n*, 17*n*–18*n*
    prominent groups after, 45
    South Korean bids to avert, 9
    South Korean public opinion on, 15
    of Soviet Union, 7
    unification following, prospects for, 14–15,
        63–67
"collapsist" view, 13, 63
colonial past, and political stability, 32, 36
commercial code, presocialist, viability of, 50*n*
communism, political-psychological coping
        response under, 44–45
communist polity
    nonrevolutionary collapse of, 12
    revolution in, 7–8
confidence index, FDI, 83
Confucian political culture, 16
constitutional succession, 44*n*
consumer products, tariffs on, 50
Convention on International Trade in
        Endangered Species, 11*n*
"cooperative engagement" scenario, 38, 40*f*,
        41, 43, 63
coping response, political-psychological, under
        communism, 44–45
corporate failures, system for, 79–81
corporate management, capital-market
        discipline on, 77–78
corporate performance, differentiation of, 79
corporate restructuring vehicle (CRV), 80
corporatist labor-market models, 82–83
corporatist political culture, 16
corruption, 61–62, 71

counterfeiting, 59
counterrevolutionaries, role after collapse, 45
CPEs. *See* centrally planned economies (CPEs)
Cuba, 12, 25, 26*t*
cultural products, South Korean, 73
currency "overhangs," 52
currency reform, 50–52, 64
Czech Republic, 8, 16

Daewoo, 76–77, 77*n*
Daewoo Motors, 80, 80*n*
Dandong, 56*n*
data appendix, 85–87
datasets, for measuring regime change, 29–30,
        34, 35*t*, 36, 86
debts, interfirm, 69
decentralization, administrative, 46
"decommunization," 12
deeding of land to tiller, 68
defector testimonies, 18
Defense Intelligence Agency, 14
de Maizière, Lothar, 4, 45
demilitarized zone (DMZ), 55, 64, 67
democracies, revolution in, 7
demographics
    data on, 85–86
    and political stability, 32
    and unification, 64
Deng Xiaoping, 17
"depoliticization," 12
deposit insurance, 79
deprivation, and possibility of collapse, 17*n*,
        19
DMZ. *See* demilitarized zone (DMZ)
drug trafficking, 59
dual-price strategy, 46–47, 49, 68
Dutch Reformed Church, 11
Duvalier, François, 27, 27*n*
Duvalier, Jean-Claude, 27

Eastern Europe. *See also specific country*
    political-psychological coping response
        under communism in, 44–45
    revolutions in, 6–8, 9, 10
"Eastern" revolution, 5
East Germany
    collapse of, 7
    unification with West Germany, 12*n*, 64–65,
        68–69
econometric measurements
    of political stability and aid, 62
    of regime change, 30, 34, 34*n*
    of transparency, 83
economic benefits, of cooperation with South
        Korea, 57–58
economic collapse, definition of, 3*n*
economic cooperation agreements, between
        North and South Korea, 55

economic distress, 21–28, 23t–24t
  duration or depth of, as measure of
    economic performance, 31
  political decisions about, 84
  and possibility of collapse, 15–16, 17n, 19
  quality of data on, 21–22, 22f
  and revolution, 9
  in selected long-lived regimes, 25, 26t, 28
economic integration, between North and
  South Korea. *See* unification
economic performance
  measuring, 29, 31–32
  and political stability, 31–33, 31n
  of South Korea, 72–83
economic reforms
  in China, 46–49, 46n, 54, 62
  July 2002 (North Korea), 46–57, 84
  components of, 46
  effect on South Korea, 60–61
  and misunderstanding of economics, 54,
    63
Economic Survey of South Korea (OECD), 81
economic union, as form of integration, 57
EEC. *See* European Economic Community
  (EEC)
Egypt, 27, 83
elite population, and revolution, 6, 10
embargo, 40–41, 40f, 43
employment, 60, 81
  in agricultural sector, 49
  data on, 85–86
engagement, economics of, 72–83
entertainment industry, South Korean, 73
Ethiopia, 5n
ethnic diversity, effect on political stability,
  32
European Economic Community (EEC), 11,
  57
European Union, 81. *See also specific country*
exchange rates, 50–52, 64
expected duration, 30
extreme-case dataset, 29–30, 35t, 36, 37f, 38
Eyadéma, Étienne (Gnassingbé), 28

famine, 9, 10
farmers' markets, 53, 53n
father-son leadership transitions, 27. *See also*
  specific leaders
Federation of Korean Industries, 15
financial health, South Korean, improvements
  in, 78–79
Financial Supervisory Commission, 76
Financial Supervisory Service (FSS), 77, 79
financial transparency, in South Korea, 76–77,
  83
Finland, 78
food aid, 61
food distribution, 48
foreign aid. *See* aid; *specific country*

foreign investment, in South Korea, 78–79,
  81–83, 81n
  barriers to, 82–83, 82n
foreign threat
  regime use of, 19
  and revolution, 5, 7–8
"forward-looking criteria," 79
France, 82
Franco, Francisco, 11
free trade area, 57
FSS. *See* Financial Supervisory Service (FSS)

gamma models, of regime change, 30, 36n
GDP growth, 22, 22f
Generally Accepted Accounting Principles
  (GAAP), 76
German unification, 12n
  versus Korean unification, 64–65, 68–69
Ghana, 27n
Global Development Network (GDN) Growth
  Database, 29, 35t, 36, 37f, 85, 87
Gorbachev, Mikhail, 7
government bond markets, 67
government-business relations, in South
  Korea, 61
government legitimacy
  and political socialization, 44–45
  in postcommunist era, 9
  public opinion of, 18
  religious basis of, 17, 19
  and revolutionary vulnerability, 10, 43
"greed" hypothesis, 32
growth rate
  data on, 85–86
  effect of unification on, 66

Haeju district, 55
Haiti, 26t, 27
hazard functions, from regime change
  regressions, 36, 37f, 38, 39f, 40–41, 40f
  data for, 87, 87t
hazard of failure, 30
heritage, and political structure, 32–33, 36
Huerta, Victoriano, 45
humanitarian aid, 61
Hungary, 8, 87
Hynix Semiconductor, 78, 80–81, 80n
Hyundai, 54–55, 58n, 61, 74–75, 75n
Hyundai Electronics, 79–80

IAS. *See* International Accounting Standards
  (IAS)
Iceland, 82
IMF. *See* International Monetary Fund (IMF)
income inequality, 60n, 66
  and unification, 65, 66
India, 83
Indonesia, 83

Infineon, 80–81
inflation
 creation of, 51–52
 data on, 85–86
 and state prices, 54
information technology, 73
insurance
 deposit, 79
 unemployment, 81
interfirm debts, 69
International Accounting Standards (IAS), 76
"international embargo" scenario, 40–41, 40f, 43
international financial organizations. *See also specific organization*
 membership in, 58–59
International Labor Organization, 11n
International Monetary Fund (IMF), 11, 22, 27n, 58
international norms, alienation from, 11, 11n
international trade, exposure to, 60n, 74
Iraq, 58
Israel, 74

Japan
 aid from, 56n, 58n
 economic integration between North Korea and, 56–57
 emperor worship in, 17
 foreign investment in South Korea from, 82
 Meiji Restoration, 5, 7
 postcolonial claims, 56, 58n, 69
Jaruzelski, Wojciech, 16
juche, 3–4, 16
 fusion with nationalism, 8–9
 modernizing reinterpretation of, 4n, 43
 public opinion of, 18
 sustainability of, 44–45

Kaesong industrial park, 55–56
Kaunda, Kenneth, 28
KEDO. *See* Korean Peninsula Energy Development Organization (KEDO)
Kenya, 26t, 27
Kenyan African National Union (KANU), 27
Kenyatta, Jomo, 27
Kerensky, Alexander, 4, 45
Kim Dae-jung, 58, 75, 75n, 82
Kim family regime
 continuation of, 4, 19, 19n, 43
 versus collapse, 2, 13–14, 44n
 effect of aid on, 61–63
Kim Il-sung, 1, 4n
 death of, predictions of collapse after, 12, 12n, 17n–18n
 as religious icon, 17, 17n
Kim Jong-il, 1–2
 reign of, predictions for, 13, 17n–18n

as religious icon, 17, 17n, 44
 sudden death of, political implications of, 44–45, 44n
 summit meeting with Kim Dae-jung, 58
Kim Jong-il regime, high-ranking members of, banishment of, 71
Kim Woo-choong, 77, 77n
Kohap, 77n
Koizumi, Junichiro, 56, 58
Korea Deposit Insurance Corporation, 77n
Korea Development Bank, 78
Korea Land Corporation (KOLAND), 55
Korean Development Bank, 61, 80n
Korean Peninsula Energy Development Organization (KEDO), 7, 56n
Korean People's Army (KPA), 3, 16
Korean Workers Party (KWP), 4n, 8, 13, 44n, 54
Kornilov, Lavr, 45
Kuran, Timur, 17

labor allocation, 47
labor laws, 81
labor migration, and unification, 64–65
labor practices, as barrier to foreign investment, 82–83, 82n
landlocked countries, economic performance of, 32
Laos, 34, 87
leaders. *See also specific leader*
 as religious icons, 16–17, 44
leadership transitions, father-son, 27
legal systems
 bankruptcy, 81
 data on, 87
 and political stability, 33, 34, 38
lending programs, multilateral development bank, 59, 59n, 69
Lenin, V.I., 17
Leninist regimes, revolutionary vulnerability of, 8, 10
LG Group, 77n
license technology, 83
loan defaults, 25, 59
"lustration" policy, 71

macroeconomic policy changes, 46
macroeconomic stability
 indicators of, 31–32
 and price structure, 50–54
 and radical integration, 65–66
Madero, Francisco, 45
Mandela, Nelson, 11, 12
Mao Tse-tung, 4n, 17
Marcos, Ferdinand, 16
marketization, 51
markets
 functioning of, 76
 "without institutions," 8

Marxism, 16
mass mobilization
    absence of institutions for, 16
    and revolution, 6–7, 8, 10
Meiji Restoration (Japan), 5, 7
microeconomic policy reforms, 46–49
Micron Technology, 80–81
Middle East, 59n
migration, and unification, 64–65
militarization
    and economic reforms, 60, 66
    and revolution, 4n, 7, 8, 10
military coordination, between the United
    States, South Korea, and China, 67–68, 72
"military-first" politics, 4, 7, 8, 47, 63
military threat, to South Korea, 45, 74
minority shareholders, 77
"miracle on the Han," 71
missiles, medium-range, exportation of, 59
Mobutu Sese Seko, 27
Moi, Daniel arap, 27
monetary conversion, dual-rate, 68
monetary union, 57, 57n, 64–65
most favored nation status, 60n
Mt. Kumgang tourism venture, 54–55
Mubarak, Hosni, 27
"muddling through," 63
Multi-Fiber Arrangement, 60n
multilateral development banks. See also
    specific bank
    lending programs, 59, 59n, 69
Muslim Brotherhood, 27

NAFTA. See North American Free Trade
    Agreement (NAFTA)
Nasser, Gamal Abdel, 27
National Defense Committee (NDC), 44n
National Democratic Party (NDP), 27
nationalism
    regime uses of, 8–9
    and revolution, 5, 7, 8–9
national myths, control of, 10, 18
national polity, as unit of political change
    analysis, 30
National Salvation Front (Romania), 25
NDC. See National Defense Committee (NDC)
neo-Confucianism, 16
"neo-conservative's dream" scenario, 40, 40f,
    41, 43
Nixon administration, 34
Nkrumah, Kwame, 27n
noncompliance, 18
normal trade relations, 60n
North American Free Trade Agreement
    (NAFTA), 57
Nuclear Non-Proliferation Treaty, 11n
nuclear reactors, 59
nuclear weapons, 56, 62, 74
null hypothesis, 34n, 36n

omitted variable bias, 31
opacity index, 83
Organization for Economic Cooperation and
    Development (OECD), 11

Palestinian Authority, 59n
"parable of the prisoner," 44
Pareto improvement, 49
Park Chung-hee, 3–4
PDS. See public distribution system (PDS)
peace dividend, 60, 66
"People's Life Bonds," 52, 52n
"People's Power" revolt, 16
People's Solidarity for Participatory
    Democracy (PSPD), 77
per capita GDP, 22, 22f
    data on, 85–86
per capita income, as measure of economic
    performance, 31
Philippines, 16
Pinochet, Augusto, 3–4
Poland, 7, 8, 16, 83
political change, 1–21. See also regime change
    abrupt, 2–12, 43, 63–69
    cross-country modeling of, 31
    gradual, 57–63
    measures of, 28–30
    probability of, estimating, 30–31
political culture, Confucian, 16
political mobilization. See also mass
    mobilization
    absence of institutions for, 16
    for nonrevolutionary change, 10
political moderates, role after collapse, 45
political rights, of North Koreans, and
    unification, 67
political socialization, 63
    and regime legitimacy, 44–45
political stability
    economic performance and, 31–33, 31n
    effects of aid on, 61–63, 62n
    modeling, 30
    and national history, 32–33, 36
political union, 57
Polity IV dataset, 29–30, 34, 35t, 36, 37f, 38, 86
pop culture, South Korean, 73
population characteristics. See demographics
poverty traps, 33
preference gap, 36
prepackaged bankruptcy (PB), 80
price structure, 47–48, 49, 53–54
    macroeconomic stability and, 50–54
PricewaterhouseCoopers, 83
privatization, 69
proletariat, and revolution, 6
property rights, 68
proportional hazard (PH) model, of regime
    change, 30, 34, 35t, 36, 36n, 37f, 38, 39f,
    40–41, 40f
    data for, 87, 87t

PSPD. *See* People's Solidarity for Participatory
Democracy (PSPD)
public distribution system (PDS), 48, 48n, 53
public opinion
of *juche* ideology, 18
of North Korea, 74
on North Korean collapse, 15
of regime legitimacy, 18
on unification, 12n–13n
Pyongyang, 6, 45, 49
Pyongyang Defense Command, 10
Pyongyang summit meeting, 58

Rajin-Sonbong region, 54, 56, 57
ration cards, 48, 48n
regime
definition of, 3, 3n
legitimacy of (*See* government legitimacy)
regime change. *See also* political change
definition of, 3, 28
gradual, 43–44, 57–63
likelihood of, 40–41, 40f
measuring, 29–30
modeling, 21–41
background on, 28–33
results of, 33–41
pace of, 43–44, 57–69
radical, 43, 63–69
use of aid to promote, 62–63, 62n
regime crisis, predictions of, 13, 38
regional dummy variables, 33
regression metrics, for regime change
measurements, 30, 34, 35t, 36
data for, 86
regulatory problems, as barrier to foreign
investment, 83
religious diversity, effect on political stability,
32
religious icons, leaders as, 16–17, 44
religious society, polity as, 16–17, 19
Republic of Korea. *See* South Korea
Research Institute for National Unification
(RINU), 13, 38
resources, underutilization of, 51
retail activity, 49
"revenue" economy, 36
revolution
definition of, 4
"Eastern," 5
"from above," 5, 7
and political ideology, 7–8
possibility of, 4–12
successful aversion of, 11–12
transaction costs of, 32
types of, 4–5
"Western," 4–6, 8
revolutionaries, role after collapse, 45
revolutionary society, indications of, 2–12
RINU. *See* Research Institute for National
Unification (RINU)

risk onset, 86
Roh Moo-hyun, 75n, 82
Romania, 6–7, 12, 25–27, 26t, 62, 83, 85
rural energy rehabilitation program, 58
Russia, 8, 83

Sachs-Warner openness index, 86
Sadat, Anwar, 27
Samsung Electronics, 80
Santong, 76–77
SAR. *See* special administrative region (SAR)
Scandinavian legal system, 34
self-reliance. *See juche*
Senate Intelligence Committee, 14
shareholders rights, 77
Singapore, 83
Sinuiju zone, 55–56
SK Group, 76, 77n
slave labor, 11n
small and medium-sized enterprises (SMEs), 55
social classes, key, alienation of, 10
social differentiation
in marketization and inflation, 51
and misappropriation of aid, 62
socialization, political, 63
and regime legitimacy, 44–45
social safety nets, 68, 81
social union, 57
South Africa, 11–12
South Korea
aid to North Korea, 58–59, 62, 65, 75
banking system, 78–79
bid to avert North Korean collapse, 9, 43,
45–46
business-government relations in, 61
economic cooperation agreements with
North Korea, 55
economic performance of, 72–83
effect of North Korean collapse on, 65–67,
75–76
effect of North Korean economic reforms
on, 60–61
financial health, improvements in, 78–79
financial transparency in, 76–77, 83
foreign investment in, 78–79, 81–83, 81n
barriers to, 82–83, 82n
implications for, 71–84
integration in world economy, 74
key role of, 43
military coordination with China and the
United States, 67–68, 72
military threat to, 45, 74
North Korean existence as antithesis of, 45,
45n
policy objectives, 74–75
at time of unification, 68–69
pop culture, 73
public opinion in
on North Korean collapse, 15
on unification, 12n–13n

public opinion of North in, 74
relations with the United States, 72
social safety net, 81
unification with North Korea (*See*
   unification)
value-added weights for, 21
Soviet system, removal of, 46*n*
Soviet Union, collapse of, 7
SPA. *See* Supreme People's Assembly (SPA)
Spain, 11
special administrative region (SAR), 55–56, 67
special economic zones, 46, 54–57. *See also*
   specific location
Stalin, Josef, 17
Stalinism, 6
Standard and Poor (S&P), 19, 74
state failure, 29*n*
state subsidies, removal of, 47
Supreme People's Assembly (SPA), 13, 15, 44*n*
Syria, 26*t*, 27

Taiwan, 74, 81
Taiwan Statistical Data Book 2003, 85
tariffs, on consumer products, 50
technological revolution, 73
technology, license, 83
terrorism, state-sponsored, 59*n*
textile exports, 60*n*
Thailand, 83
"Thai model," 2, 43
"third way" policy package, 46*n*
"tier three/semi-transparent" category, 83
Timisoara (Romania), 6
Togo, 26*t*, 28
Tontons Macoutes (Haiti), 27, 27*n*
"too big to fail" theory, 80–81, 80*n*
tourism venture (Mt. Kumgang), 54–55
trade exposure, 60*n*, 74
trade protection measures, calculation of,
   86–87
transaction costs, of revolution, 32
transitional country category, 33
transition paths, 43–69
transparency, 75–77, 83
transparency risk premium, 83
Tripartite Commission, 82, 83
tropical climate, and political stability, 32, 36
Turkey, 5, 83
Turkmenistan, 8, 12

underutilization of resources, 51
unemployment insurance, 81
unification
   and "cooperative engagement" scenario, 43
   costs of, 19, 45, 65–66
   forcible effort at, 64
   forms of, 57

versus German unification, 64–65, 68–69
   pace of, 1, 43, 57–69
   and political rights of North Koreans, 67
   predictions of, 12*n*–13*n*, 43
   prospects for, 14–15, 63–64
   public opinion on, 12*n*–13*n*
   South Korean policy objectives at, 68–69
unification bonds, 67
unionization rates, 82
United Kingdom, 83
United States
   1994 Agreed Framework with North Korea,
      15, 59
   aid from, 18, 58, 58*n*, 62
   military coordination with South Korea and
      China, 67–68, 72
   North Korean claims against, 60
   policy on North Korea, 45–46
   relations with South Korea, 72
   trade with, 60*n*
   transparency level of, 83
urbanization
   data on, 85–86
   effect on political stability, 32
urban population, and revolution, 6, 10
Uzbekistan, 8, 12

value-added weights, South Korean, 21
Vietnam, 12, 44, 49, 59

wages, 47, 49, 51
   and unification attempts, 64–65
wealth inequality, 60*n*, 66
weapon sales, 59
Weibull function, 30, 34*n*, 36*n*
"Western" revolution, 4–6, 8
West Germany, unification with East
   Germany, 12*n*, 64–65, 68–69
WFP. *See* World Food Program (WFP)
"winner" firms, 79
won (North Korean)
   "foreigner's," 52
   "people's," 52
   value of, 50–52, 68
World Bank, 22, 56, 58, 59*n*
   datasets from, 29, 34, 85–86
   Global Development Network Growth
      Database, 85, 87
   political stability categories, 33
World Food Program (WFP), 48, 51

Yang Bin, 55

Zambia, 26*t*, 27, 28
"zombie" firms, 79

Other Publications from the Institute for International Economics

* = out of print

POLICY ANALYSES IN
INTERNATIONAL ECONOMICS Series

1 The Lending Policies of the International
   Monetary Fund*   John Williamson
   August 1982   ISBN 0-88132-000-5
2 "Reciprocity": A New Approach to World
   Trade Policy?*   William R. Cline
   September 1982   ISBN 0-88132-001-3
3 Trade Policy in the 1980s*
   C. Fred Bergsten and William R. Cline
   November 1982   ISBN 0-88132-002-1
4 International Debt and the Stability of the
   World Economy*   William R. Cline
   September 1983   ISBN 0-88132-010-2
5 The Exchange Rate System,* Second Edition
   John Williamson
   Sept. 1983, rev. June 1985 ISBN 0-88132-034-X
6 Economic Sanctions in Support of Foreign
   Policy Goals*
   Gary Clyde Hufbauer and Jeffrey J. Schott
   October 1983   ISBN 0-88132-014-5
7 A New SDR Allocation?*   John Williamson
   March 1984   ISBN 0-88132-028-5
8 An International Standard for Monetary
   Stabilization*   Ronald L. McKinnon
   March 1984   ISBN 0-88132-018-8
9 The Yen/Dollar Agreement: Liberalizing
   Japanese Capital Markets*   Jeffrey A. Frankel
   December 1984   ISBN 0-88132-035-8
10 Bank Lending to Developing Countries: The
   Policy Alternatives*   C. Fred Bergsten,
   William R. Cline, and John Williamson
   April 1985   ISBN 0-88132-032-3
11 Trading for Growth: The Next Round of
   Trade Negotiations*
   Gary Clyde Hufbauer and Jeffrey J. Schott
   September 1985   ISBN 0-88132-033-1
12 Financial Intermediation Beyond the Debt
   Crisis*   Donald R. Lessard, John Williamson
   September 1985   ISBN 0-88132-021-8
13 The United States-Japan Economic Problem*
   C. Fred Bergsten and William R. Cline
   October 1985, 2d ed. January 1987
                          ISBN 0-88132-060-9
14 Deficits and the Dollar: The World Economy
   at Risk*   Stephen Marris
   December 1985, 2d ed. November 1987
                          ISBN 0-88132-067-6

15 Trade Policy for Troubled Industries*
   Gary Clyde Hufbauer and Howard R. Rosen
   March 1986   ISBN 0-88132-020-X
16 The United States and Canada: The Quest for
   Free Trade*   Paul Wonnacott, with an
   appendix by John Williamson
   March 1987   ISBN 0-88132-056-0
17 Adjusting to Success: Balance of Payments
   Policy in the East Asian NICs*
   Bela Balassa and John Williamson
   June 1987, rev. April 1990 ISBN 0-88132-101-X
18 Mobilizing Bank Lending to Debtor
   Countries*   William R. Cline
   June 1987   ISBN 0-88132-062-5
19 Auction Quotas and United States Trade
   Policy*   C. Fred Bergsten, Kimberly Ann
   Elliott, Jeffrey J. Schott, and Wendy E. Takacs
   September 1987   ISBN 0-88132-050-1
20 Agriculture and the GATT: Rewriting the
   Rules*   Dale E. Hathaway
   September 1987   ISBN 0-88132-052-8
21 Anti-Protection: Changing Forces in United
   States Trade Politics*
   I. M. Destler and John S. Odell
   September 1987   ISBN 0-88132-043-9
22 Targets and Indicators: A Blueprint for the
   International Coordination of Economic
   Policy
   John Williamson and Marcus H. Miller
   September 1987   ISBN 0-88132-051-X
23 Capital Flight: The Problem and Policy
   Responses*   Donald R. Lessard and
   John Williamson
   December 1987   ISBN 0-88132-059-5
24 United States-Canada Free Trade: An
   Evaluation of the Agreement*
   Jeffrey J. Schott
   April 1988   ISBN 0-88132-072-2
25 Voluntary Approaches to Debt Relief*
   John Williamson
   Sept.1988, rev. May 1989 ISBN 0-88132-098-6
26 American Trade Adjustment: The Global
   Impact*   William R. Cline
   March 1989   ISBN 0-88132-095-1
27 More Free Trade Areas?*
   Jeffrey J. Schott
   May 1989   ISBN 0-88132-085-4
28 The Progress of Policy Reform in Latin
   America*   John Williamson
   January 1990   ISBN 0-88132-100-1
29 The Global Trade Negotiations: What Can Be
   Achieved?*   Jeffrey J. Schott
   September 1990   ISBN 0-88132-137-0
30 Economic Policy Coordination: Requiem or
   Prologue?*   Wendy Dobson
   April 1991   ISBN 0-88132-102-8

31 The Economic Opening of Eastern Europe*
John Williamson
May 1991 ISBN 0-88132-186-9

32 Eastern Europe and the Soviet Union in the World Economy*
Susan M. Collins and Dani Rodrik
May 1991 ISBN 0-88132-157-5

33 African Economic Reform: The External Dimension* Carol Lancaster
June 1991 ISBN 0-88132-096-X

34 Has the Adjustment Process Worked?*
Paul R. Krugman
October 1991 ISBN 0-88132-116-8

35 From Soviet disUnion to Eastern Economic Community?*
Oleh Havrylyshyn and John Williamson
October 1991 ISBN 0-88132-192-3

36 Global Warming The Economic Stakes*
William R. Cline
May 1992 ISBN 0-88132-172-9

37 Trade and Payments After Soviet Disintegration* John Williamson
June 1992 ISBN 0-88132-173-7

38 Trade and Migration: NAFTA and Agriculture* Philip L. Martin
October 1993 ISBN 0-88132-201-6

39 The Exchange Rate System and the IMF: A Modest Agenda Morris Goldstein
June 1995 ISBN 0-88132-219-9

40 What Role for Currency Boards?
John Williamson
September 1995 ISBN 0-88132-222-9

41 Predicting External Imbalances for the United States and Japan*William R. Cline
September 1995 ISBN 0-88132-220-2

42 Standards and APEC: An Action Agenda*
John S. Wilson
October 1995 ISBN 0-88132-223-7

43 Fundamental Tax Reform and Border Tax Adjustments* Gary Clyde Hufbauer
January 1996 ISBN 0-88132-225-3

44 Global Telecom Talks: A Trillion Dollar Deal*
Ben A. Petrazzini
June 1996 ISBN 0-88132-230-X

45 WTO 2000: Setting the Course for World Trade Jeffrey J. Schott
September 1996 ISBN 0-88132-234-2

46 The National Economic Council: A Work in Progress * I. M. Destler
November 1996 ISBN 0-88132-239-3

47 The Case for an International Banking Standard Morris Goldstein
April 1997 ISBN 0-88132-244-X

48 Transatlantic Trade: A Strategic Agenda*
Ellen L. Frost
May 1997 ISBN 0-88132-228-8

49 Cooperating with Europe's Monetary Union
C. Randall Henning
May 1997 ISBN 0-88132-245-8

50 Renewing Fast Track Legislation* I. M.Destle
September 1997 ISBN 0-88132-252-0

51 Competition Policies for the Global Economy
Edward M. Graham and J. David Richardson
November 1997 ISBN 0-88132 -249-0

52 Improving Trade Policy Reviews in the Worle Trade Organization Donald Keesing
April 1998 ISBN 0-88132-251-2

53 Agricultural Trade Policy: Completing the Reform Timothy Josling
April 1998 ISBN 0-88132-256-3

54 Real Exchange Rates for the Year 2000
Simon Wren Lewis and Rebecca Driver
April 1998 ISBN 0-88132-253-9

55 The Asian Financial Crisis: Causes, Cures, and Systemic Implications Morris Goldstein
June 1998 ISBN 0-88132-261-X

56 Global Economic Effects of the Asian Currency Devaluations
Marcus Noland, LiGang Liu, Sherman Robinson, and Zhi Wang
July 1998 ISBN 0-88132-260-1

57 The Exchange Stabilization Fund: Slush Money or War Chest? C. Randall Henning
May 1999 ISBN 0-88132-271-7

58 The New Politics of American Trade: Trade, Labor, and the Environment
I. M. Destler and Peter J. Balint
October 1999 ISBN 0-88132-269-5

59 Congressional Trade Votes: From NAFTA Approval to Fast Track Defeat
Robert E. Baldwin and Christopher S. Magee
February 2000 ISBN 0-88132-267-9

60 Exchange Rate Regimes for Emerging Markets: Reviving the Intermediate Option
John Williamson
September 2000 ISBN 0-88132-293-8

61 NAFTA and the Environment: Seven Years Later Gary Clyde Hufbauer, Daniel Esty, Diana Orejas, Luis Rubio, and Jeffrey J. Schott
October 2000 ISBN 0-88132-299-7

62 Free Trade between Korea and the United States? Inbom Choi and Jeffrey J. Schott
April 2001 ISBN 0-88132-311-X

63 New Regional Trading Arrangements in the Asia Pacific?
Robert Scollay and John P. Gilbert
May 2001 ISBN 0-88132-302-0

64 Parental Supervision: The New Paradigm for Foreign Direct Investment and Development
Theodore H. Moran
August 2001 ISBN 0-88132-313-6

55 The Benefits of Price Convergence:
Speculative Calculations
Gary Clyde Hufbauer, Erika Wada,
and Tony Warren
December 2001   ISBN 0-88132-333-0
56 Managed Floating Plus
Morris Goldstein
March 2002   ISBN 0-88132-336-5
57 Argentina and the Fund: From Triumph
to Tragedy
Michael Mussa
July 2002   ISBN 0-88132-339-X
58 East Asian Financial Cooperation
C. Randall Henning
September 2002   ISBN 0-88132-338-1
59 Reforming OPIC for the 21st Century
Theodore H. Moran
May 2003   ISBN 0-88132-342-X
70 Awakening Monster: The Alien Tort
Statute of 1789
Gary C. Hufbauer and Nicholas Mitrokostas
July 2003   ISBN 0-88132-366-7
71 Korea after Kim Jong-il
Marcus Noland
January 2004   ISBN 0-88132-373-X

BOOKS

IMF Conditionality* John Williamson, editor
1983   ISBN 0-88132-006-4
Trade Policy in the 1980s* William R. Cline, editor
1983   ISBN 0-88132-031-5
Subsidies in International Trade*
Gary Clyde Hufbauer and Joanna Shelton Erb
1984   ISBN 0-88132-004-8
International Debt: Systemic Risk and Policy
Response*   William R. Cline
1984   ISBN 0-88132-015-3
Trade Protection in the United States: 31 Case
Studies* Gary Clyde Hufbauer, Diane E. Berliner,
and Kimberly Ann Elliott
1986   ISBN 0-88132-040-4
Toward Renewed Economic Growth in Latin
America* Bela Balassa, Gerardo M. Bueno, Pedro-
Pablo Kuczynski, and Mario Henrique Simonsen
1986   ISBN 0-88132-045-5
Capital Flight and Third World Debt*
Donald R. Lessard and John Williamson, editors
1987   ISBN 0-88132-053-6
The Canada-United States Free Trade Agreement:
The Global Impact*
Jeffrey J. Schott and Murray G. Smith, editors
1988   ISBN 0-88132-073-0
World Agricultural Trade: Building a Consensus*
William M. Miner and Dale E. Hathaway, editors
1988   ISBN 0-88132-071-3
Japan in the World Economy*
Bela Balassa and Marcus Noland
1988   ISBN 0-88132-041-2

America in the World Economy: A Strategy for
the 1990s*   C. Fred Bergsten
1988   ISBN 0-88132-089-7
Managing the Dollar: From the Plaza to the
Louvre*   Yoichi Funabashi
1988, 2nd ed. 1989   ISBN 0-88132-097-8
United States External Adjustment and the World
Economy* William R. Cline
May 1989   ISBN 0-88132-048-X
Free Trade Areas and U.S. Trade Policy*
Jeffrey J. Schott, editor
May 1989   ISBN 0-88132-094-3
Dollar Politics: Exchange Rate Policymaking in
the United States*
I.M. Destler and C. Randall Henning
September 1989   ISBN 0-88132-079-X
Latin American Adjustment: How Much Has
Happened?*   John Williamson, editor
April 1990   ISBN 0-88132-125-7
The Future of World Trade in Textiles and
Apparel* William R. Cline
1987, 2d ed. June 199 ISBN 0-88132-110-9
Completing the Uruguay Round: A Results-
Oriented Approach to the GATT Trade
Negotiations* Jeffrey J. Schott, editor
September 1990   ISBN 0-88132-130-3
Economic Sanctions Reconsidered (2 volumes)
Economic Sanctions Reconsidered:
Supplemental Case Histories
Gary Clyde Hufbauer, Jeffrey J. Schott, and
Kimberly Ann Elliott
1985, 2d ed. Dec. 1990   ISBN cloth 0-88132-115-X
                         ISBN paper 0-88132-105-2
Economic Sanctions Reconsidered: History and
Current Policy
Gary Clyde Hufbauer, Jeffrey J. Schott, and
Kimberly Ann Elliott
December 1990   ISBN cloth 0-88132-140-0
                         ISBN paper 0-88132-136-2
Pacific Basin Developing Countries: Prospects for
the Future*   Marcus Noland
January 1991   ISBN cloth 0-88132-141-9
                         ISBN paper 0-88132-081-1
Currency Convertibility in Eastern Europe*
John Williamson, editor
October 1991   ISBN 0-88132-128-1
International Adjustment and Financing: The
Lessons of 1985-1991* C. Fred Bergsten, editor
January 1992   ISBN 0-88132-112-5
North American Free Trade: Issues and
Recommendations*
Gary Clyde Hufbauer and Jeffrey J. Schott
April 1992   ISBN 0-88132-120-6
Narrowing the U.S. Current Account Deficit*
Allen J. Lenz
June 1992   ISBN 0-88132-103-6
The Economics of Global Warming
William R. Cline/June 1992 ISBN 0-88132-132-X

U.S. Taxation of International Income: Blueprint for Reform*   Gary Clyde Hufbauer, assisted by Joanna M. van Rooij
October 1992   ISBN 0-88132-134-6
Who's Bashing Whom? Trade Conflict in High-Technology Industries   Laura D'Andrea Tyson
November 1992   ISBN 0-88132-106-0
Korea in the World Economy*   Il SaKong
January 1993   ISBN 0-88132-183-4
Pacific Dynamism and the International Economic System*
C. Fred Bergsten and Marcus Noland, editors
May 1993   ISBN 0-88132-196-6
Economic Consequences of Soviet Disintegration*
John Williamson, editor
May 1993   ISBN 0-88132-190-7
Reconcilable Differences? United States-Japan Economic Conflict*
C. Fred Bergsten and Marcus Noland
June 1993   ISBN 0-88132-129-X
Does Foreign Exchange Intervention Work?
Kathryn M. Dominguez and Jeffrey A. Frankel
September 1993   ISBN 0-88132-104-4
Sizing Up U.S. Export Disincentives*
J. David Richardson
September 1993   ISBN 0-88132-107-9
NAFTA: An Assessment
Gary Clyde Hufbauer and Jeffrey J. Schott/ rev. ed.
October 1993   ISBN 0-88132-199-0
Adjusting to Volatile Energy Prices
Philip K. Verleger, Jr.
November 1993   ISBN 0-88132-069-2
The Political Economy of Policy Reform
John Williamson, editor
January 1994   ISBN 0-88132-195-8
Measuring the Costs of Protection in the United States
Gary Clyde Hufbauer and Kimberly Ann Elliott
January 1994   ISBN 0-88132-108-7
The Dynamics of Korean Economic Development*   Cho Soon
March 1994   ISBN 0-88132-162-1
Reviving the European Union*
C. Randall Henning, Eduard Hochreiter, and Gary Clyde Hufbauer, editors
April 1994   ISBN 0-88132-208-3
China in the World Economy   Nicholas R. Lardy
April 1994   ISBN 0-88132-200-8
Greening the GATT: Trade, Environment, and the Future   Daniel C. Esty
July 1994   ISBN 0-88132-205-9
Western Hemisphere Economic Integration*
Gary Clyde Hufbauer and Jeffrey J. Schott
July 1994   ISBN 0-88132-159-1
Currencies and Politics in the United States, Germany, and Japan
C. Randall Henning
September 1994   ISBN 0-88132-127-3

Estimating Equilibrium Exchange Rates
John Williamson, editor
September 1994   ISBN 0-88132-076-5
Managing the World Economy: Fifty Years After Bretton Woods   Peter B. Kenen, editor
September 1994   ISBN 0-88132-212-1
Reciprocity and Retaliation in U.S. Trade Policy
Thomas O. Bayard and Kimberly Ann Elliott
September 1994   ISBN 0-88132-084-6
The Uruguay Round: An Assessment*
Jeffrey J. Schott, assisted by Johanna W. Buurman
November 1994   ISBN 0-88132-206-7
Measuring the Costs of Protection in Japan*
Yoko Sazanami, Shujiro Urata, and Hiroki Kawai
January 1995   ISBN 0-88132-211-3
Foreign Direct Investment in the United States, 3d ed., Edward M. Graham and Paul R. Krugman
January 1995   ISBN 0-88132-204-0
The Political Economy of Korea-United States Cooperation*
C. Fred Bergsten and Il SaKong, editors
February 1995   ISBN 0-88132-213-X
International Debt Reexamined* William R. Cline
February 1995   ISBN 0-88132-083-8
American Trade Politics, 3d ed., I.M. Destler
April 1995   ISBN 0-88132-215-6
Managing Official Export Credits: The Quest for a Global Regime*   John E. Ray
July 1995   ISBN 0-88132-207-5
Asia Pacific Fusion: Japan's Role in APEC*
Yoichi Funabashi
October 1995   ISBN 0-88132-224-5
Korea-United States Cooperation in the New World Order*
C. Fred Bergsten and Il SaKong, editors
February 1996   ISBN 0-88132-226-1
Why Exports Really Matter!* ISBN 0-88132-221-0
Why Exports Matter More!* ISBN 0-88132-229-0
J. David Richardson and Karin Rindal
July 1995; February 1996
Global Corporations and National Governments
Edward M. Graham
May 1996   ISBN 0-88132-111-7
Global Economic Leadership and the Group of Seven   C. Fred Bergsten and C. Randall Henning
May 1996   ISBN 0-88132-218-0
The Trading System After the Uruguay Round*
John Whalley and Colleen Hamilton
July 1996   ISBN 0-88132-131-1
Private Capital Flows to Emerging Markets After the Mexican Crisis*   Guillermo A. Calvo, Morris Goldstein, and Eduard Hochreiter
September 1996   ISBN 0-88132-232-6
The Crawling Band as an Exchange Rate Regime: Lessons from Chile, Colombia, and Israel
John Williamson
September 1996   ISBN 0-88132-231-8

Flying High: Liberalizing Civil Aviation in the
Asia Pacific*
Gary Clyde Hufbauer and Christopher Findlay
November 1996   ISBN 0-88132-227-X
Measuring the Costs of Visible Protection
in Korea*   Namdoo Kim
November 1996   ISBN 0-88132-236-9
The World Trading System: Challenges Ahead
Jeffrey J. Schott
December 1996   ISBN 0-88132-235-0
Has Globalization Gone Too Far?   Dani Rodrik
March 1997   ISBN cloth 0-88132-243-1
Korea-United States Economic Relationship*
C. Fred Bergsten and Il SaKong, editors
March 1997   ISBN 0-88132-240-7
Summitry in the Americas: A Progress Report
Richard E. Feinberg
April 1997   ISBN 0-88132-242-3
Corruption and the Global Economy
Kimberly Ann Elliott
June 1997   ISBN 0-88132-233-4
Regional Trading Blocs in the World Economic
System   Jeffrey A. Frankel
October 1997   ISBN 0-88132-202-4
Sustaining the Asia Pacific Miracle:
Environmental Protection and Economic
Integration Andre Dua and Daniel C. Esty
October 1997   ISBN 0-88132-250-4
Trade and Income Distribution   William R. Cline
November 1997   ISBN 0-88132-216-4
Global Competition Policy
Edward M. Graham and J. David Richardson
December 1997   ISBN 0-88132-166-4
Unfinished Business: Telecommunications after
the Uruguay Round
Gary Clyde Hufbauer and Erika Wada
December 1997   ISBN 0-88132-257-1
Financial Services Liberalization in the WTO
Wendy Dobson and Pierre Jacquet
June 1998   ISBN 0-88132-254-7
Restoring Japan's Economic Growth
Adam S. Posen
September 1998   ISBN 0-88132-262-8
Measuring the Costs of Protection in China
Zhang Shuguang, Zhang Yansheng, and Wan
Zhongxin
November 1998   ISBN 0-88132-247-4
Foreign Direct Investment and Development:
The New Policy Agenda for Developing
Countries and Economies in Transition
Theodore H. Moran
December 1998   ISBN 0-88132-258-X
Behind the Open Door: Foreign Enterprises in the
Chinese Marketplace
Daniel H. Rosen
January 1999   ISBN 0-88132-263-6

Toward A New International Financial
Architecture: A Practical Post-Asia Agenda
Barry Eichengreen
February 1999   ISBN 0-88132-270-9
Is the U.S. Trade Deficit Sustainable?
Catherine L. Mann
September 1999   ISBN 0-88132-265-2
Safeguarding Prosperity in a Global Financial
System: The Future International Financial
Architecture, Independent Task Force Report
Sponsored by the Council on Foreign Relations
Morris Goldstein, Project Director
October 1999   ISBN 0-88132-287-3
Avoiding the Apocalypse: The Future of the
Two Koreas   Marcus Noland
June 2000   ISBN 0-88132-278-4
Assessing Financial Vulnerability: An Early
Warning System for Emerging Markets
Morris Goldstein, Graciela Kaminsky, and Carmen
Reinhart
June 2000   ISBN 0-88132-237-7
Global Electronic Commerce: A Policy Primer
Catherine L. Mann, Sue E. Eckert, and Sarah
Cleeland Knight
July 2000   ISBN 0-88132-274-1
The WTO after Seattle   Jeffrey J. Schott, editor
July 2000   ISBN 0-88132-290-3
Intellectual Property Rights in the Global
Economy   Keith E. Maskus
August 2000   ISBN 0-88132-282-2
The Political Economy of the Asian Financial
Crisis   Stephan Haggard
August 2000   ISBN 0-88132-283-0
Transforming Foreign Aid: United States
Assistance in the 21st Century   Carol Lancaster
August 2000   ISBN 0-88132-291-1
Fighting the Wrong Enemy: Antiglobal Activists
and Multinational Enterprises Edward M.Graham
September 2000   ISBN 0-88132-272-5
Globalization and the Perceptions of American
Workers
Kenneth F. Scheve and Matthew J. Slaughter
March 2001   ISBN 0-88132-295-4
World Capital Markets: Challenge to the G-10
Wendy Dobson and Gary C. Hufbauer,
assisted by Hyun Koo Cho
May 2001   ISBN 0-88132-301-2
Prospects for Free Trade in the Americas
Jeffrey J. Schott
August 2001   ISBN 0-88132-275-X
Toward a North American Community:
Lessons from the Old World for the New
Robert A. Pastor
August 2001   ISBN 0-88132-328-4
Measuring the Costs of Protection in Europe:
European Commercial Policy in the 2000s
Patrick A. Messerlin
September 2001   ISBN 0-88132-273-3

Job Loss from Imports: Measuring the Costs
Lori G. Kletzer
September 2001   ISBN 0-88132-296-2
No More Bashing: Building a New Japan–United
States Economic Relationship   C. Fred Bergsten,
Takatoshi Ito, and Marcus Noland
October 2001   ISBN 0-88132-286-5
Why Global Commitment Really Matters!
Howard Lewis III and J. David Richardson
October 2001   ISBN 0-88132-298-9
Leadership Selection in the Major Multilaterals
Miles Kahler
November 2001   ISBN 0-88132-335-7
The International Financial Architecture:
What's New? What's Missing?   Peter Kenen
November 2001   ISBN 0-88132-297-0
Delivering on Debt Relief: From IMF Gold to
a New Aid Architecture
John Williamson and Nancy Birdsall,
with Brian Deese
April 2002   ISBN 0-88132-331-4
Imagine There's No Country: Poverty, Inequality,
and Growth in the Era of Globalization
Surjit S. Bhalla
September 2002   ISBN 0-88132-348-9
Reforming Korea's Industrial Conglomerates
Edward M. Graham
January 2003   ISBN 0-88132-337-3
Industrial Policy in an Era of Globalization:
Lessons from Asia
Marcus Noland and Howard Pack
March 2003   ISBN 0-88132-350-0
Reintegrating India with the World Economy
T.N. Srinivasan and Suresh D. Tendulkar
March 2003   ISBN 0-88132-280-6
After the Washington Consensus:
Restarting Growth and Reform in
Latin America   Pedro-Pablo Kuczynski
and John Williamson, editors
March 2003   ISBN 0-88132-347-0
The Decline of US Labor Unions and
the Role of Trade   Robert E. Baldwin
June 2003   ISBN 0-88132-341-1
Can Labor Standards Improve under
Globalization?
Kimberly Ann Elliott and Richard B. Freeman
June 2003   ISBN 0-88132-332-2
Crimes and Punishments? Retaliation
under the WTO
Robert Z. Lawrence
October 2003   ISBN 0-88132-359-4
Inflation Targeting in the World Economy
Edwin M. Truman
October 2003   ISBN 0-88132-345-4
Foreign Direct Investment and Tax
Competition   John H. Mutti
November 2003   ISBN 0-88132-352-7

SPECIAL REPORTS

1   Promoting World Recovery: A Statement on
    Global Economic Strategy*
    by Twenty-six Economists from Fourteen Countri
    December 1982   ISBN 0-88132-013-7
2   Prospects for Adjustment in Argentina,
    Brazil, and Mexico: Responding to the Debt
    Crisis*   John Williamson, editor
    June 1983   ISBN 0-88132-016-1
3   Inflation and Indexation: Argentina, Brazil,
    and Israel*   John Williamson, editor
    March 1985   ISBN 0-88132-037-4
4   Global Economic Imbalances*
    C. Fred Bergsten, editor
    March 1986   ISBN 0-88132-042-0
5   African Debt and Financing*
    Carol Lancaster and John Williamson, editors
    May 1986   ISBN 0-88132-044-7
6   Resolving the Global Economic Crisis: After
    Wall Street*
    by Thirty-three Economists from Thirteen
    Countries
    December 1987   ISBN 0-88132-070-6
7   World Economic Problems*
    Kimberly Ann Elliott and John Williamson,
    editors
    April 1988   ISBN 0-88132-055-2
    Reforming World Agricultural Trade*
    by Twenty-nine Professionals from Seventeen
    Countries
    1988   ISBN 0-88132-088-9
8   Economic Relations Between the United
    States and Korea: Conflict or Cooperation?*
    Thomas O. Bayard and Soogil Young, editors
    January 1989   ISBN 0-88132-068-4
9   Whither APEC? The Progress to Date and
    Agenda for the Future*
    C. Fred Bergsten, editor
    October 1997   ISBN 0-88132-248-2
10 Economic Integration of the Korean
    Peninsula
    Marcus Noland, editor
    January 1998   ISBN 0-88132-255-5
11 Restarting Fast Track*
    Jeffrey J. Schott, editor
    April 1998   ISBN 0-88132-259-8
12 Launching New Global Trade Talks:
    An Action Agenda   Jeffrey J. Schott, editor
    September 1998   ISBN 0-88132-266-0
13 Japan's Financial Crisis and Its Parallels to
    US Experience
    Ryoichi Mikitani and Adam S. Posen, eds.
    September 2000   ISBN 0-88132-289-X
14 The Ex-Im Bank in the 21st Century: A New
    Approach?   Gary Clyde Hufbauer and Rita
    M. Rodriguez, editors
    January 2001   ISBN 0-88132-300-4

15 The Korean Diaspora in the World
   Economy
   C. Fred Bergsten and Inbom Choi, eds.
   January 2003   ISBN 0-88132-358-6
16 Dollar Overvaluation and the World
   Economy
   C. Fred Bergsten and John Williamson, eds.
   February 2003   ISBN 0-88132-351-9

WORKS IN PROGRESS

A Radical Transformation of the European
Economy
Martin Neil Baily
New Regional Arrangements and the World
Economy
C. Fred Bergsten
The Globalization Backlash in Europe and
the United States
C. Fred Bergsten, Pierre Jacquet, and Karl Kaiser
Has Globalization Gone Far Enough?
Scott Bradford and Robert Z. Lawrence
Trade Policy and Global Poverty
William R. Cline
China's Entry into the World Economy
Richard N. Cooper
The ILO in the World Economy
Kimberly Ann Elliott
Reforming Economic Sanctions
Kimberly Ann Elliott, Gary C. Hufbauer,
and Jeffrey J. Schott
Cooperation Between the IMF and the
World Bank
Michael Fabricius
Currency Mismatching in Emerging Markets
Morris Goldstein and Philip Turner
NAFTA: A Ten-Year Appraisal
Gary C. Hufbauer and Jeffrey J. Schott
New Agricultural Negotiations in
the WTO
Tim Josling and Dale Hathaway

Food Regulation and Trade: Toward a Safe
and Open Global System
Tim Josling, Donna Roberts, and David Orden
Workers at Risk: Job Loss from Apparel,
Textiles, Footwear, and Furniture
Lori G. Kletzer
Responses to Globalization: US Textile
and Apparel Workers and Firms
Lori Kletzer, James Levinsohn, and
J. David Richardson
Making the Rules: Case Studies on
US Trade Negotiation
Robert Z. Lawrence, Charan Devereaux,
and Michael Watkins
US-Egypt Free Trade Agreement
Robert Z. Lawrence and Ahmed Galal
High Technology and the Globalization
of America
Catherine L. Mann
International Financial Architecture
Michael Mussa
Germany and the World Economy
Adam S. Posen
Chasing Dirty Money: Progress on
Anti-Money Laundering
Peter Reuter and Edwin M. Truman
Global Forces, American Faces:
US Economic Globalization at the
Grass Roots
J. David Richardson
US-Taiwan FTA Prospects
Daniel H. Rosen and Nicholas R. Lardy
Private Sector Investment and
Debt Workouts
Nouriel Roubini and Brad Setser
Free Trade Agreements: US Strategies
and Priorities
Jeffrey J. Schott, editor
Curbing the Boom-Bust Cycle
John Williamson

DISTRIBUTORS OUTSIDE THE UNITED STATES

**Australia, New Zealand,
and Papua New Guinea**
D.A. Information Services
648 Whitehorse Road
Mitcham, Victoria 3132, Australia
tel: 61-3-9210-7777
fax: 61-3-9210-7788
email: service@adadirect.com.au
http://www.dadirect.com.au

Canada
Renouf Bookstore
5369 Canotek Road, Unit 1
Ottawa, Ontario KlJ 9J3, Canada
tel: 613-745-2665
fax: 613-745-7660
http://www.renoufbooks.com

United Kingdom and Europe
(including Russia and Turkey)
The Eurospan Group
3 Henrietta Street, Covent Garden
London WC2E 8LU England
tel: 44-20-7240-0856
fax: 44-20-7379-0609
http://www.eurospan.co.uk

India, Bangladesh, Nepal, and Sri Lanka
Viva Books Pvt.
Mr. Vinod Vasishtha
4325/3, Ansari Rd.
Daryaganj, New Delhi-110002
India
tel: 91-11-327-9280
fax: 91-11-326-7224
email: vinod.viva@gndel.globalnet.
ems.vsnl.net.in

Japan and the Republic of Korea
United Publishers Services, Ltd.
KenkyuSha Bldg.
9, Kanda Surugadai 2-Chome
Chiyoda-Ku, Tokyo 101 Japan
tel: 81-3-3291-4541
fax: 81-3-3292-8610
email: saito@ups.co.jp
**For trade accounts only.
Individuals will find IIE books in
leading Tokyo bookstores.**

Southeast Asia (Brunei, Cambodia,
China, Malaysia, Hong Kong, Indonesia,
Laos, Myanmar, the Philippines, Singapore,
Taiwan, and Vietnam)
Hemisphere Publication Services
1 Kallang Pudding Rd. #0403
Golden Wheel Building
Singapore 349316
tel: 65-741-5166
fax: 65-742-9356

Thailand
Asia Books
5 Sukhumvit Rd. Soi 61
Bangkok 10110 Thailand
tel: 662-714-07402 Ext: 221, 222, 223
fax: 662-391-2277
email: purchase@asiabooks.co.th
http://www.asiabooksonline.com

**Visit our Web site at:
www.iie.com
E-mail orders to:
orders@iie.com**